# THE great new zealand CAFÉ

**MATTHEW HAWKE & NIKI GRENNELL**

## THANKS

This book would not have become a reality without the help of many special people. From friends and family, to supportive sponsors — they helped this venture become a reality. Along the way we met some amazing café owners and stayed at wonderful places; Niki and I have many fond memories that we will treasure for life. Thank you to all the people in the coffee industry who willingly gave us their time and their hospitality, helping to build this story. Matthew would particularly like to thank Sandra, for without her unexpected generosity the great photos in this book would have been much harder to take. To the elusive Mark McCarthy for showing us that being over 50 means you can have a 1950s-style motorbike, make fashion T-shirts with skulls on them and still look cool. To Bharti for the tent and Dennis and Noelene who believed in us and kept the positive momentum going when at times we wanted to give up. Many thanks to New Holland Publishers and to all the companies that made this adventure possible; Honda New Zealand, Huhtamaki, BNI, Auckland Camera and Moa. And don't forget to visit our website www.pukuart.co.nz.

First published in 2011 by New Holland Publishers (NZ) Ltd
Auckland • Sydney • London • Cape Town

www.newhollandpublishers.co.nz

218 Lake Road, Northcote, Auckland 0627, New Zealand
Unit 1, 66 Gibbes Street, Chatswood, NSW 2067, Australia
86–88 Edgware Road, London W2 2EA, United Kingdom
80 McKenzie Street, Cape Town 8001, South Africa

Copyright © 2011 in text: Matthew Hawke and Niki Grennell
Copyright © 2011 in photography: Matthew Hawke and Niki Grennell
Copyright © 2011 New Holland Publishers (NZ) Ltd
Matthew Hawke and Niki Grennell have asserted their rights to be identified as the authors of this work.

ISBN: 978 1 86966 319 3

Publishing manager: Christine Thomson
Editor: Caroline Budge
Design: Nick Turzynski, redinc, Auckland

Front cover: From top to bottom; Café Nina; Groove Kitchen Espresso; Café Rhombus.
Back cover: From top to bottom; Lambretta's Café & Bar; C1 Espresso; Food at Wharepuke.

A catalogue record for this book is available from the National Library of New Zealand.

10 9 8 7 6 5 4 3 2 1

Colour reproduction by Pica Digital Pte, Singapore
Printed in China by Toppan Leefung Printing Ltd, on paper sourced from sustainable forests.

All rights reserved. No part of this publication may be reproduced, stored in a retrieval system, or transmitted in any form or by any means, electronic, mechanical, photocopying, recording or otherwise, without the prior permission of the publishers and copyright holders.

While every care has been taken to ensure the information contained in this book is as accurate as possible, the authors and publishers can accept no responsibility for any loss, injury or inconvenience sustained by any person using the advice contained herein.

# CONTENTS

**Introduction 4**
**Map: Our Trip Across NZ 6**
**Cafés 8**
    Exploring the west: Cambridge to Kaikoura 8
    Rounding the south: Nelson to Amberley 20
    Returning to the north: Wellington to Auckland 80

**History of Coffee 58**
**Roasting 82**
**Where to next? 140**
**Acknowledgements 140**

# INTRODUCTION

Having written and published our first book *Espresso Escape*, a journey around Auckland's cafés, the idea of a New Zealand-wide one seemed daunting. How could we fund it; were there enough great cafés? We needed a publisher; we weren't prepared to do the amount of work to self-publish again. Yet serendipity is a strange occurrence — a phone call out of the blue finds our publisher, and after a year of planning we are off to explore New Zealand's character cafés. We follow the same simple guideline as for our first book — the cafés have to be recommended by people who love their coffee: baristas, café owners and passionate locals.

We stretch the perceptions of what defines a traditional family. Niki has two children, Mika and Ruby. Matthew has a son, Ethan. Each of us has had previous serious relationships that have produced ex-partners and these children. Okay, that part is not too complicated. But add to the mix that our children span English, Maori, Samoan and Korean cultures, and that the adults in the mix all get along and respect each other — as do the children — then at times the logistics of who should be where are a nightmare.

But we love the experience that these circumstances and rich cultures give us; even in those times when we wish it was easier, we believe that is what family is all about — learning to live with each other, warts and all.

As a country we have been drinking coffee since the early 19th century, possibly earlier. An explosion of café culture and the introduction of the flat white led to us creating a unique culture that we are proud of. New Zealand is arguably the best country in the world to visit and do a café crawl, exploring cafés and countryside that will take your breath away. From the top of the North Island to the bottom of the South, there are beautiful mountains, rivers and beaches, with cafés around them making your favourite coffee. From shipping container to garden centre; a man's hallway to a place on a cliff top that a flying fox takes you to (no cars allowed), cafés are now as much a part of Kiwi culture as are fish and chips and jandals. We have embraced a drink that originated in Europe, blended and ground it to be our own, and created a cultural identity that sets the scene for the rest of the world to follow — Go New Zealand . . .

You can read this book in three ways:
- enjoy following our journey as we visit the many great character cafés across the land;
- open the book at random, pick a destination and head off on your own adventure;
- or, if by chance you are lucky enough to be travelling already, then this book can be used as a guide. We showcase a café in most destinations you will visit, and some you may not have heard of.

When reading this book you will notice that we don't always comment on the food. The reason for this is simple: our goal is to provide you with a feel for the overall experience of visiting these cafés. It is a given that the coffee and food will be good. Niki has managed cafés, and Matthew has visited cafés across the world; between them they have over 60 years' experience of café culture. If the café isn't up to scratch, then it isn't in this book.

The food ranges from bought-in muffins and pastries to freshly made on-site creations. The cafés we visited where the food was exceptional we tell you about. Some had such good food that we managed to get the recipe and have included them in this book so you can sample it for yourself.

At the beginning of each entry, we name the coffee roast each café serves. There is a wide range available around the country, from the well-known, such as Supreme, to lesser known roasts, like Bay Espresso. For us they all have a passion and it comes down to personal taste.

Most of all, we want you to enjoy and share the celebration we were a part of for a few months. Get to know New Zealand's coffee history, and how we came to be a country of many roasters, but most importantly enjoy reading about the unique character of New Zealand's people and what we do with coffee . . .

   Enjoy.

# OUR TRIP ACROSS NZ

- LAMBRETTA'S CAFÉ & BAR 28
- JESTER HOUSE CAFÉ 30
NELSON

REID'S STORE CAFÉ
MARUIA 26

- BEACH HOUSE CAFÉ 22
- HISLOPS WHOLEFOODS CAFÉ 24
KAIKOURA

PICTON TO WELLINGTON COOK STRAIT FERRY

DP:ONE CAFÉ
GREYMOUTH 32

- NOR'WESTER CAFÉ
AMBERLEY 78

- UNDER THE RED VERANDAH 68
- C1 ESPRESSO 70
- SWEETHEARTS AT BERRYFIELDS 76
CHRISTCHURCH

BUSHMAN'S CENTRE CAFÉ
PUKEKURA 34

DUNSANDEL STORE
DUNSANDEL 72

PRIMO E SECUNDO
METHVEN 74

LYTTELTON COFFEE COMPANY
LYTTELTON 66

MAKARORA COUNTRY CAFÉ
MAKARORA 36

KAHU CAFÉ
OMARAMA 62

ARTHUR ST CAFÉ
TIMARU 64

THE GLENORCHY CAFÉ
GLENORCHY 42

PROVISIONS
ARROWTOWN 38

VESTA
QUEENSTOWN 40

THE PACKHOUSE
ROXBURGH 44

- CHUCKY'S COFFEE HOUSE 54
- STRICTLY COFFEE COMPANY 56
- THE PORT ROYALE CAFÉ 60
DUNEDIN

MRS CLARK'S CAFÉ
RIVERTON 48

LEES DAIRY & CAFÉ
WYNDHAM 50

STICKY BEAK CAFÉ
INVERCARGILL 46

CATLINS CAFÉ
OWAKA 52

WELLINGTON TO PICTON COOK STRAIT FERRY

The day has finally arrived — the day that we leave Auckland, heading on a three-month adventure across New Zealand, our only guide a café list. The sun is shining as we head south over the Bombay Hills, the sprawl of the large metropolis behind us. Each one of us is excited and there is a song in the air, along with the ubiquitous car game 'I spy'. Feeling relaxed away from the big city, we drive through Cambridge and over a very narrow bridge (trucks not allowed) towards the first café — one the owner calls a destination café.

# LILY PAD CAFÉ

**1242 Kaipaki Road**
**CAMBRIDGE**

### ROCKET

We arrive at the Lily Pad Café during the busiest time of day. Owner Kate Ward, who must tire of people thinking she is too young to own such a business, is working flat out in the kitchen, so Niki positions herself at the window to the kitchen, interviewing Kate while she cooks up a storm.

Kate is extremely organised and capable. While talking to Niki she not only manages the kitchen as head chef, but keeps an eye on the floor, making suggestions to the floor staff, as well as flitting out to deal with a demanding customer. And all the while the food that leaves the kitchen looks delectable, positively mouth-watering from our 'too busy to eat' vantage point.

This is definitely a destination café, and The Garden Art Studio next door is an excellent complementary business. **One of the things we loved was the places to look through — shuttered windows opening to the fields, cleverly manicured hedges to give glimpses of the café as you arrive,** and the open-ended building which adds to the inside/outside flow.

The café offers seafood evenings and Tapas nights. Live music is also becoming more of a feature, and Kate's dad Max is part of a band that can be seen playing in the café on the occasions he escapes from duty as the trusty dishwasher!

If you choose to make your way to the Lily Pad Café you're in for some great food. Our favourite meal to go out for — breakfast — is available all day. Just don't turn up on a Monday as that is their day of rest . . . otherwise, enjoy.

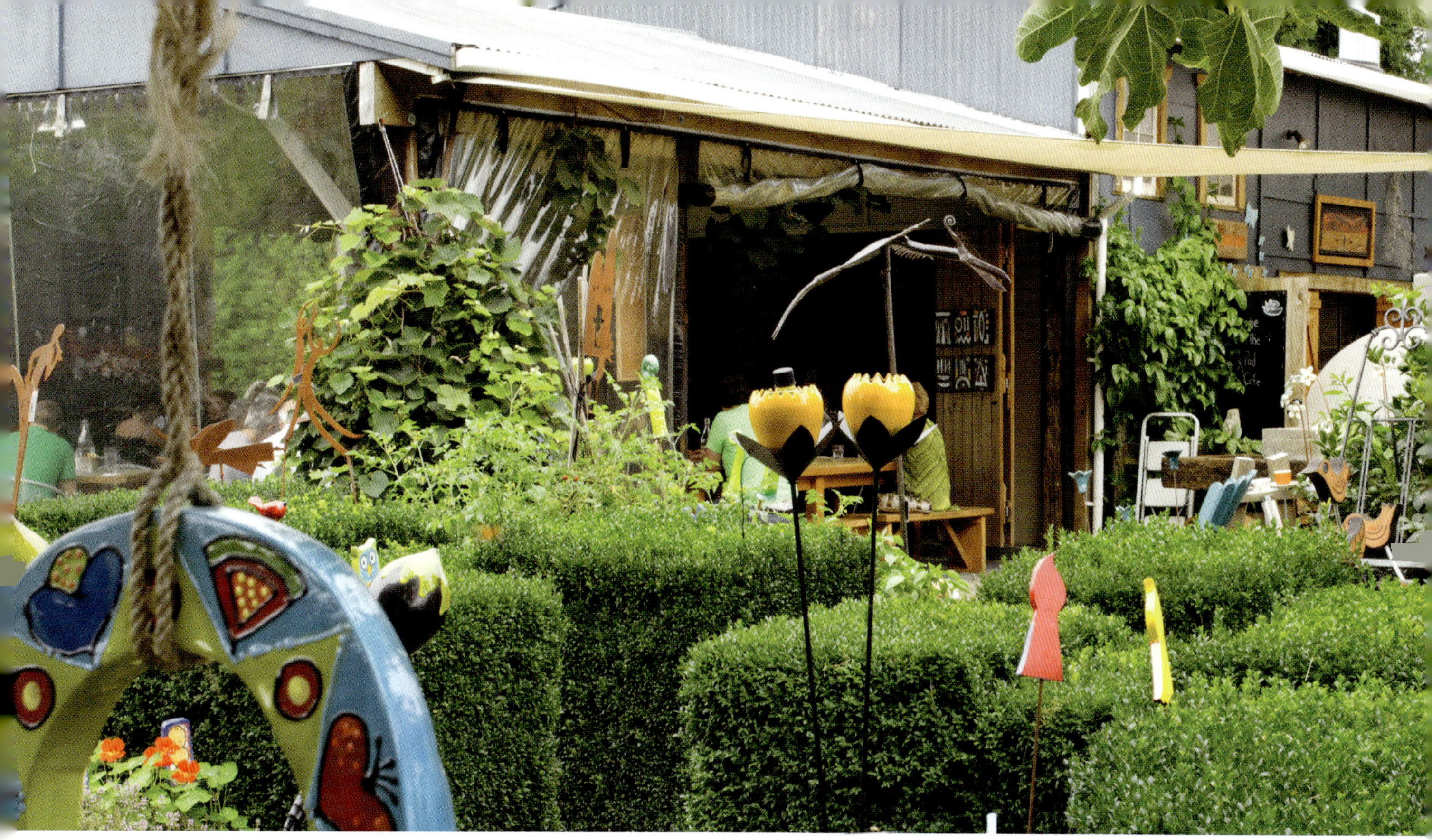

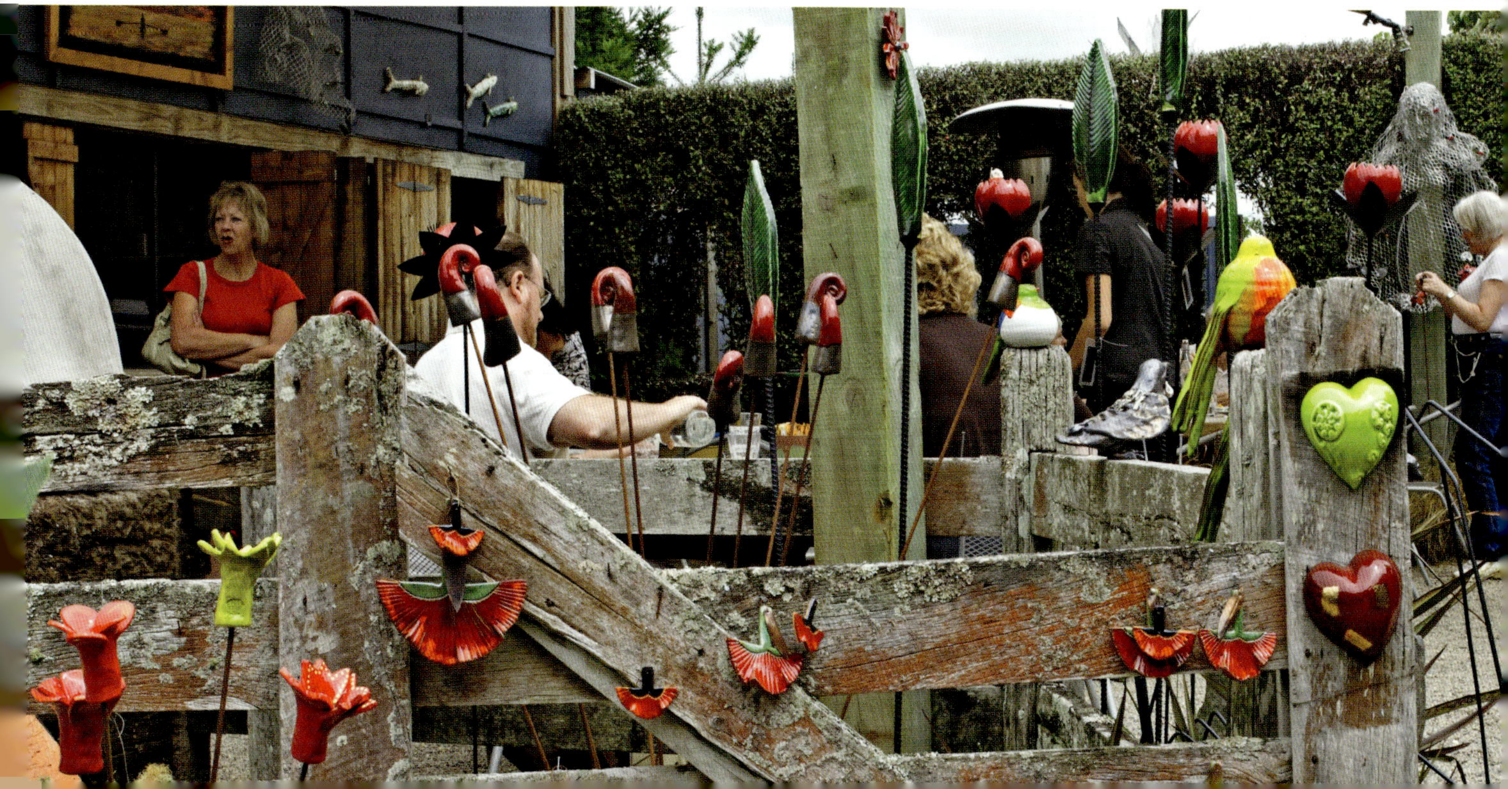

Having successfully completed our first feature café, it's time to head to Waitomo for some fun with the kids. Black water rafting is on the menu. Our accommodation for the night has been recommended as being great for kids. It is called Woodlyn Park, and what makes it stand out from other motels is the choice of accommodation on offer — you can stay in a ship, airplane, train, or even a Hobbit house. We end up in the ship and have a great stay — with no seasickness. Having slept well, we awake to a day of cafés. Passing Otorohanga railway station, we come across a sign for Origin Coffee, and decide to investigate.

# ORIGIN COFFEE STATION

**7 Wahanui Crescent**
**OTOROHANGA, 200 METRES OFF STATE HIGHWAY 3**

## ORIGIN

The Origin Coffee Station is part of an operational station where trains will stop on request, but the interior has been taken over by Malawian immigrant Roger Sheppard for his own little coffee haven. He roasts once or twice a week, depending on demand, and offers an overview of how the coffee reaches its devotees — from plant to cup. There are beans growing in the station and barista training on offer for those who want to improve the standard of their home brew.

Back in Malawi, Roger worked on a plantation growing coffee. His responsibility was to sample-roast and taste the beans, monitoring the quality for the customers buying the raw product. He and his wife Liz moved to New Zealand around the millennium to find better schooling for their kids and to get away from malaria. They had brought some coffee beans from Malawi for their own use. Roger would roast them and take them to dinner parties in lieu of wine. Those who were lucky enough to receive encouraged Roger to expand on the roasting, and eventually the Origin Coffee Station came to town. The beans are still sourced from Malawi.

Origin Coffee Station does not offer meals; cakes and slices are available and you are most welcome to bring your own food. **The focus here is the coffee, and it was a great coffee to start the day with. The train station is a bonus, and if you sit a while and have a chat you are sure to learn something about our burgeoning national drink that you didn't know before.**

We leave Otorohanga with a good taste in our mouths, and that satisfied feeling of finding an unexpected treat. Our next stop is well off the beaten track, far from a major highway — take this road for so long then look for the green bridge, then look for the red one. After what seems like an hour of driving along gravel roads, we arrive at one of our most memorable experiences of the whole trip, the Blue Duck Lodge.

# BLUE DUCK CAFÉ

**Blue Duck Lodge, 4265 Oio Road**
**WHAKAHORO RD 2, OWHANGO 3990**

### VOLCANO COFFEE

You wouldn't think it possible to find a decent café in such an isolated place, but we do. We arrive tired and a little 'windy road wobbly' to a great reception: food, coffee, puppies, and a baby goat alongside a bird that (briefly) stuns itself flying into a café window.

The café is but a small part of what is going on in this stunning area of the Whakahoro Valley, near the banks of the Whanganui River. Dan Steele is the man with the passion and vision who has allowed nature to recreate a little piece of paradise — what was here before man made his mark. Dan is mad keen on the whio or blue duck and has made it his mission to recreate their habitat and eradicate the predators that are cutting down their numbers to just 600 breeding pairs left in New Zealand.

The Irish couple behind the counter multi-task in the extreme — during our stay there they do everything from cooking to organising a digger rescue and taking out a hunting mission. Although the coffee is of the plunger variety, which may put off some purists, Matthew enjoys the best plunger latte ever. The food is made to order and served with love.

With the weather looking dodgy for the following day we decide to take up the offer of looking around the station that afternoon. We climb aboard a Polaris, a kind of overdone four-wheel-drive golf cart, along with five madly excited dogs! We blast along farm tracks, past buildings that were abandoned along with the farms when given to returned servicemen from the First World War as reward for their contribution. No wonder they abandoned them — most of the land is vertical and covered in bush.

Hot and dusty, we end up standing at the top of a waterfall leading down into a waterhole. We walk on down, and kayaking and swimming are enjoyed by all. We never manage to catch sight of a blue duck, but the look of joy on the kids' faces as we race around is what this journey is about — giving the kids the experience of a lifetime. **The Blue Duck Café and Lodge is officially very high up on our list as a favourite all-round experience.**

Feeling revived after being surrounded by the best of New Zealand, it is time for a long drive to New Plymouth. Deciding on the not-so-main route we travel along the Forgotten World Highway, a rugged, surprisingly busy 150-kilometre stretch of road between Taumarunui in the north and Stratford in the south. On the way we travel through the Republic of Whangamomona — a 40-strong settlement that celebrates its very own Independence Day every January — strange and eerie tunnels, and some stunning scenery of the volcanic plateaus of the central North Island and the snow-capped Mt Taranaki.

Arriving in New Plymouth it's time for more cafés, and our first is Bach on Breakwater — a great place to come for dinner as the sun is setting. The next day we take a long, long walk along the waterfront to look for the Big Wave Café. We go past the famous Wind Wand — a narrow red fibreglass tube that reaches 45 metres into the air and can bend in the wind. Then we see what we've been looking for — the local icon of the Big Wave Café. Imagine for a moment that you are in the most comfortable retro chair in a quintessential Kiwi bach (crib for the southern reader), watching the world pass by. As you stare out at the vista, children playing on the beach, you are drinking a more than reasonable coffee and eating some fantastic food. In New Plymouth that dream is realised at the Big Wave Café.

# THE BIG WAVE CAFÉ

**Along the beach**
**NEW PLYMOUTH**

## OZONE

This café came from the busy mind of Mike Welsh, while waiting for the surf to come in at Piha. Combining his skill as a marine engineer turned luxury mobile home builder with a love of good food and coffee, the result is a mobile café in the shape of the perfect wave. Piha was not ready for him but New Plymouth was; hence they are a lucky population.

Mike is originally from Christchurch and has a love of surfing, as is evident in the surfboards that multi-task as both tables and menu boards for this outdoor experience. The whole set-up is mobile, to keep in line with the deal they have with the local council. Seven days a week (weather dependent), everything is arranged in the early morning and disassembled at varying times of the late afternoon or early evening, depending on demand. To be available to do this Mike and his wife Michelle live in the camping ground close by. But don't feel that they are missing out in any way. As has been established, Mike is a dab hand at building luxury motor homes; they have a spa on the roof of theirs.

Although Michelle wasn't around at the conception of The Big Wave, her input has been invaluable. Mike tends to be the ideas man while Michelle sets up the structures to facilitate those ideas into fruition. It's taken a lot of hard work; mistakes have been made and trial and error has been a big part of the learning curve. But with experience has come a flow, and they are now in a position to look into possibly franchising a successful model.

The day we visit it is a real treat. We have pizza that is sublime and emerges from a space that looks too small for cooking such wonders (they don't have a microwave). The kids play in the river and on the beach for hours while we drink coffee and watch them. We also take in the locals walking the waterfront, many with dogs who welcome the dog biscuits and fresh water that are always on offer. **The Big Wave combines the comfort of a holiday-home chair — complete with blanket on cooler days — with the surf culture that goes hand in hand with New Plymouth, and coffee and food to go out of your way for . . . Yay.**

From the beach town of New Plymouth it's time to head towards the river and visit Whanganui. We have heard of a café on the way that's named after the kids' favourite drink; we wonder what it will be like. The drive is fairly typical, with mile after mile of paddocks. Matthew has to stop and take a photo, something that by the end of the trip we will all be a little sick of. Eventually we come to the town of Opunake, our latest café awaiting us for lunch.

# SUGAR JUICE CAFÉ

**42–44 Tasman Street**
**OPUNAKE**

### SUPREME

The name encapsulates everything that Beth Hunt and Jarrah Edge want to have in their food and café experience — juicy and sweet. **Nutritious food made with love is the base; add in a garden and top it off with local art — dished out with a little quirk for good measure.**

'Sugar' is the resident mannequin, acquired from Wards Department Store in New Plymouth. The details of her arrival are filed under 'don't ask, won't tell'. Now, though, she is dressed to suit any local occasion or event and takes pride of place in the town parade. She must be the most loved and attended-to family-friendly mannequin in the country.

Beth is originally from Pohutu and Jarrah from Whanganui. Years ago Beth used one of the two shop fronts the café now takes up as a health food shop. She and Jarrah met while working overseas and eventually a business partnership was formed, with Jarrah as chef and Beth the master baker in the expanded business of Sugar Juice Café back on home turf. Some of Beth's food dates back to the health food store days and she makes the lightest, tastiest wholemeal pastry Niki has ever had. Gluten-free and vegetarian options abound.

Although Sugar Juice entices many a passing traveller, their main business is local and they have a big connection with the community. Many of the staff have been with the café almost from the beginning. One of the great things about cafés in small-town New Zealand is the employment they provide in an often barren job market. Gwyneth, one of the long-term employees, lives at the local lighthouse her father tended in days gone by. She's adamant that the success of Sugar Juice is due more to its heart than to the fabulous food. Sugar Juice pays homage to the fantastic surf beaches in the area by naming

all the breakfasts after the best surf spots. You can get dinner here also, from Wednesday through to Saturday.

After lunch we head across the road and down to the beach for a swim. The kids especially enjoy the park and shallow pool. Cafés are fun for kids, especially when sweet treats are on offer, but beaches and parks are better! Arriving in Whanganui (or is it Wanganui?), we have a number of cafés that have been recommended, such as The Pukeko's Nest Café and Reflections Café, but the one that really takes our fancy has a catch. We can't get there by car. And so we settle into the Whanganui River Top 10 Holiday Park — a beautiful spot by the river where the kids have time to unwind, and we have a chance to organise a barbecue. The next day we head off to the café, but not by car. This is a café that stretches the description of café as you may think of it, but if we didn't tell you about it you would be worse off. Dan from the Blue Duck put us onto this place, and we have a fantastic time going way off the beaten track.

# THE FLYING FOX

**on the Whanganui River**
**SOUTH OF KORINITI, 3081 WHANGANUI RIVER ROAD**
**OR, CONTACT SPIRIT OF THE RIVER JET, HAVOC @ FOX TOUR**

### HAVOC

The Flying Fox retreat accommodation and café is not an easy place to access. If you want the café experience you need to get on board the *Spirit of the River* jetboat and make your way up-river. Either that, or go across on the flying fox. **The peace, beauty, muffins and coffee that greet you on arrival only add to the novelty and serenity of the journey.**
The property's owned by John and Annette Main, but this has not always been the case; their retreat accommodation is built on ancestral lands that used to be a Maori pa. John and Annette see themselves as kaitiaki or guardians of the land, and local Maori have given them their blessing and support. In between tangata whenua and the Mains, the land was cleared to grow tobacco and wheat, not successfully by all accounts as the farming family walked off the land.

Not so far from the property is what is left of Jerusalem, the spiritual community that James K Baxter was a part of. In honour of his memory, the Flying Fox has a James K Baxter cottage available for rent.

The gardens are certified organic and the muffins on offer sublime. Annette used to cook gourmet feasts for guests, but the food was so good that numbers increased and it became too much of a drain on the couple's other commitments and interests.

Niki has travelled New Zealand extensively and seen many a long drop on her travels; however, the view from the Flying Fox long drop is a treat and the facility itself pretty stylish. The kids are a little taken aback but manage as there are no other options. They enjoy collecting the free-range eggs and having a go on the flying fox itself. There is a tinge of disappointment that it's not a sit and hang on for dear life variety, but they are entertained nonetheless.

While we enjoy all that is on offer, we bump into a group about to go kayaking down the river. The opportunity for photos and the abundance of history available make the whole experience rich. The café may not fit the city image, but good food and coffee was had by all.

From the bush of the Flying Fox to the style of Wellington — we are headed to the port to catch the Interislander across to the South Island. Niki has been travelling on the ferry since childhood as a means of visiting family in the south for Christmas. Many a good memory of the excitement of getting a drink and food on a moving ship has been had. The joy of walking away from Mum and Dad with money in hand for one of the first tastes of independence is still able to be felt.

We are booked on an early sailing so we can take a look at Café Oliveto on the ferry. After the well rehearsed rush to not miss the sailing we take a seat in the family lounge and explore from there. In Niki's childhood coffee was of the Cona filter variety and by today's standards left much to be desired. Things have changed. Thankfully.

At this time of morning the bar is chocka, and it would seem that the days of serving alcohol are gone. Men who look like they would be at home with a beer in hand have their caffeine of choice instead.

Café Oliveto also has a fast moving queue, all awaiting the first coffee of the day. The baristas on board compete between themselves. They have a high standard and quick hands as over 1000 coffees go out to the travellers on each sailing. No café in the country has the buzz of travel alongside ever-changing scenery that makes the Interisland Ferry a unique café experience.

Arriving at Picton is an exciting experience; watching the nooks and crannies of the harbour as the ferry sails in. We are summoned to our cars and before we know it are driving and headed for Kaikoura. We pass the famous Nin's Bin — a caravan that's been selling fresh crayfish and mussels since the 1970s, with the stunning coast as a backdrop. We shortly arrive in Kaikoura and see a café that looks like it could be worth a look.

# BEACH HOUSE CAFÉ

**39A Beach Road**
**KAIKOURA**

## LOCAL ROAST

The café is on the main road into Kaikoura from the north, set in what was originally a local home. The building has been adjusted for its current purpose, yet there is a real feeling of walking into a lounge to visit with friends. Even better, they have a tamariki room so you can visit with the adults while the kids get down in a toy- and couch-filled separate space. Wayne and Coral Thomas are local to Kaikoura and after a time in their own café in Hawke's Bay they decided to make their way home and set up shop . . . shops actually. Family and friends are the focus here, with all of the Thomas girls working in the café at times making coffee and keeping the customers happy.

There are tables out the front and the back, all of which are sporadically watched over by Sid, the canine chief in charge of seagull dispersion. Sid and Mika become firm friends instantly, which according to Wayne is the way of Sid. He either loves you or shows indifference on sight. Indifference bordering on dislike is directed at Niki, as Sid leaves the premises as soon as she pays him any attention.

**Wayne and Coral have a philosophy that others would do well to emulate: that everyone who walks through the door should be treated equally, and the service they receive should be consistent.** Family takes priority, and keeping things simple while living in the moment is key. We took from here memories of good food and coffee along with some reminders of what life is really about.

We spend the night across the road and the next day do what all tourists do in Kaikoura — we go and look for whales. We board a boat, head out to sea, and it isn't long before we see our first whale, well at least its tail. The crew know almost to the second when a whale is likely to surface so you have a good chance of seeing one. Add to this the other sea life and dolphins swimming with us, and the experience is well worth taking the kids on. Arriving back in Kaikoura we pop into Hislops Wholefoods Café to complete our café jaunt for Kaikoura, and learn of a real slice of New Zealand history.

# HISLOPS WHOLEFOODS CAFÉ

**33 Beach Road**
**KAIKOURA 7300**

## ALLPRESS

It is not surprising that Paul and Elizabeth Hislop are heading up a café with the word wholefood in the title, when you discover their family connections with organics. Paul was born and raised in Kaikoura by parents who had a lot to do with the beginning of the organic movement. Paul's dad was soliciting farmers to grow food without chemicals as early as the 1950s. Wwoofers, the term used for people who work on organically oriented properties in return for food and lodgings, were the first to suggest the idea of a café to the family. **It would build on the existence of their organic flour mill, vegetable growing and bee hives. This home-grown produce, along with eggs and herbs, are still used in the current café fare.**

Hislops Wholefoods Café was established in 1995 in the leased building. In 2007 they bought the building and reinvented themselves by adding catering and use of the building for functions. In November 2010 they launched their latest persona as a wine bar that intends to provide a range of wines which are organic as much as is possible. This, in addition to bread-making, cooking and coffee-training classes, makes Hislops a busy and educational place.

One thing that may be a little new for the average café patron is the table service. The Hislops have travelled extensively and are attracted to the table service they received in France and Italy particularly. The Kiwi consumer is more used to counter service in a café, and this can cause confusion. Once we all get the hang of what is supposed to happen, the seasonal food and slick décor give rise to a pleasurable, healthy experience.

# HISLOPS WHOLEFOODS CAFÉ'S **CARROT CAKE**

4 cups carrots
2 cups Hislops wholemeal flour
1 teaspoon cinnamon
1 teaspoon mixed spices
¾ cup sultanas
¾ cup currants
½ cup pumpkin seeds
½ cup sunflower seeds
¼ cup sliced almonds
1 cup shredded coconut

5 eggs
1 cup grapeseed oil
¾ cup brown sugar
¾ cup raw sugar
1 teaspoon vanilla essence
1 cup dried apricots
½ cup brazil nuts
3 teaspoons baking soda

**ICING**
750g cream cheese
2 cups icing sugar
1 teaspoon vanilla essence

Preheat oven to 180°C. In a food processor grate the carrots, and then put into a large stainless steel bowl. Add the flour, cinnamon, mixed spices, sultanas, currants, pumpkin seeds, sunflower seeds, sliced almonds and coconut. Mix with a large spoon. In the food processor put eggs, oil, sugars and vanilla essence. Mix thoroughly. Add apricots, brazil nuts and baking soda, and pulse until chopped and mixed. Add this mixture to the dry ingredients and mix well. Spoon into a 30 cm cake pan lined with baking paper. Bake for one hour then check at 10-minute intervals until cooked.

Beat all the icing ingredients together or blend in food processor until smooth. Add more icing sugar as necessary. Decorate with chopped apricots and pumpkin seeds.

This is a large cake so save it for the family gathering or work 'do', unless of course you and yours have puku that can keep on receiving.

From the coastal beauty of Kaikoura we travel inland and spend a night at Hanmer Springs before heading to Murchison and on to Nelson the next day. On the way we make a lunch stop at Reid's Store in Maruia. The name is said to mean sheltered or shady in te reo Maori and is known to be a rest stop used historically by Maori and Pakeha alike.

# REID'S STORE CAFÉ

**State Highway 65**
**MARUIA**

**VIVACE**

The Reids who opened the original store way back in 1929 provided shelter and goods for those travelling along State Highway 65 in a way that is consistent with old-time hospitality. Doug Reid was known to open up the petrol pumps for unprepared travellers in the middle of the night without complaint. His son still comes in every day for his newspaper, and it seems he approves of what current owners Mark Rogers and Karen Stewart have created from the old family business.

Mark and Karen are not local. Mark hails from Christchurch and Karen from further afield, Scotland. On returning to New Zealand from the United Kingdom, the couple went searching for a business they could afford in an area that appealed. They came upon the store and spent ten months renovating the property themselves. Originally they had an accommodation component to the building, but as the café became busier and busier this became too much and they concentrated solely on the café business.

Reid's Store Café is located in the CBD of Maruia, along with the school and community hall. There are about 80 households in the valley and the café is a local meeting place that is used for special occasions too. Much of the business takes place over the summer months, with holiday makers heading for the Nelson Lakes district stopping along the way. **Mark and Karen want their café to be a stop and linger experience, and also a convenient stop for those who want to grab and continue on their journey.** The food reflects this with a varied cabinet along with menu items. The location of the store makes supply more difficult than the city cafés have to deal with. An up-side is that everything is made on site from scratch.

Summer is not only the time for travellers. The local sandflies are in

abundance in the evenings and when there is cloud cover. An organic insect repellent is on hand for those whose blood is the sweetest. Luckily we arrived on one of those scorching 30-degree, clear-sky days and were not under attack. During winter things slow down considerably and the café is closed on Tuesday, Wednesday and Thursday.

    The kids enjoy the rope swing and manage to find some of the more risqué items that are tucked away on the packed shelves of things to buy.

Nelson has plenty of artists and those who choose an alternative lifestyle, but they are joined by a much more mainstream majority, arguably good or bad, and — thankfully — by Lambretta's Café and Bar.

# LAMBRETTA'S CAFÉ & BAR

**204 Hardy Street
NELSON**

## POMEROY'S

Lambretta's was started by an original group of four that has reduced to the current owners, couple Rhys Odey and Leanne Murray. Together they have the café and two small boys. Anyone who has parented knows the workload involved — and the same can be said for anyone who has run a café. Leanne and Rhys have huge energy levels, especially apparent in Rhys. This man can talk, and move, and watch the café floor, and notice what is going on in the kitchen, and provide the perfect drinks without prompting for our growly children, all without taking attention away from explaining the history of the café.

Lambretta's was set up in time for the new millennium, with a number of locals being fans since day one. One man has been coming in every second day without fail over that eleven-year timeframe. **Why do they come? Well, it could be the food that is freshly made on the premises every day. There's not a fried item in sight and the only thing that comes through the door in its completed form are the custard squares from Denheath bakery.** The salads are a treat for the eyes and the taste buds, and there's a most gorgeous smell as you walk through the door.

The Italian theme came about with both the building and having pizza as the food staple in the beginning. The scooters came next, with the first rather memorably acquired from a bike gang in Blenheim. There are now a number of scooters mounted on the wall, and sitting outside by the front steps.

We have a ball here, with lots for Ruby to do in the courtyard. Kids' toys are tucked away in a manner that encourages putting away and the rocking scooter seems to get a lot of use. Lambretta's was smoke free before it became law, and this kind of innovation is what keeps this long-time café fresh and contemporary. It's obviously an international favourite, and a favourite for us too. By the way, don't forget to try the chilli jam.

# LAMBRETTA'S CROSTATA

2 cups flour
½ cup sugar
240 g cold cubed butter
2 tablespoons cold water
1 cup fresh or frozen raspberries
1 cup drained tinned peaches
Juice of ½ a lemon
1 tablespoon sugar

1 egg
1 tablespoon sugar

Preheat oven to 180°C. Process flour, sugar, butter and water in a food processer until it forms a ball; do not let it get warm. Roll out this pastry into a circle on baking paper to about 4 mm depth and place on a baking tray.

In a bowl mix the raspberries and peaches with the lemon juice and the first measure of sugar. Spread the fruit mix on the centre of the pastry, leaving a 3 cm border around the outside.

Fold up the edges of the pastry so the juice does not leak out.

Brush the pastry with the beaten egg and sprinkle with the second measure of sugar. Bake for 30–40 minutes.

Lambretta's is right in the heart of Nelson, so getting a bit out into the country is our next port of call. We hear the king Jester is in the house.

# JESTER HOUSE CAFÉ & TAME EELS

**320 Aporo Road
COASTAL HIGHWAY, TASMAN 7152**

### POMEROY'S

Try this philosophy for creating a great café and lifestyle: **within a culture of excellence, sustainability and funism (a McGillicuddy Serious Party term, we believe), it is as easy to make good food as bad; may as well make good food.**

This is how Judy and Steve Richards have steered their business and life since they arrived from farming in Canterbury 20 years ago. Initially they lived in the back of the 1930s corrugated iron cottage and ran the café from the front. From this humble beginning they have transformed what was a bare paddock into a spectacular and often edible garden. They have their own orchard, boasting apples, pears, citrus . . . the list goes on. Fresh herbs abound and they grow their own lavender for the extra special lavender shortbread.

In 1995 it became time to build a house on the property to accommodate the growing kids and growing café. The buildings and grounds are ever-evolving and each visit is met by a new creation in progress. To some the sheer work involved in such a project would be insurmountable. Not for Judy and Steve. They don't watch television and don't commute to work, so a lot more time is available than for most. Alongside their own toils, the efforts of Wwoofers have helped create this little piece of paradise.

Judy and Steve called their creation Jester for a very specific reason. They are passionate about sharing a more sustainable way of living with whoever they can. The idea is that historically the Jester was able to deliver an uncomfortable message to the king without having his head removed. The message that the Richards deliver may be uncomfortable for some to hear, but the delivery makes it palatable.

Steve and Judy are firm believers that being sustainable and 'green' is efficient and, in the long term, cost-effective. Most of the café waste is dealt with on site, with only one bin of plastic wrap and bottles that needs to be taken away per fortnight. Produce is sourced locally, the paint is eco paint that lasts for 300 years, beer comes in kegs only and juice in glass bottles. The toilets are of the composting variety; and yet this café is on its way to creating a new stereotypical image for green — that of slick, quality and nourishing fare.

We couldn't talk about Jester House without mentioning the eels. As the official name suggests, they are tame and our kids take great pleasure in feeding them with the eel food you can buy. The eels slide up on to the rocks and will allow gentle touching. One last thing: if you are looking for a romantic getaway in a building shaped like a shoe, this is where you will find it. The shoe house is only for the grown-ups and at a discreet distance from the action.

## JESTER'S **LAVENDER SHORTBREAD**

**220 g chopped chilled butter**
**¾ cup caster sugar**
**2 cups flour**
**½ cup rice flour**
**1 egg**
**1 tablespoon dried lavender buds**

Preheat oven to 160°C. Process butter, caster sugar, flour, rice flour and egg in a food processor until smooth.

Place on a lightly floured surface and knead gently. While kneading, add the lavender buds.

Roll into balls and place on a baking tray lined with baking paper. Flatten each ball gently with a floured fork.

Bake for 20 minutes.

Makes about 35 biscuits.

We spend a night in Motueka with family before heading south and down the West Coast. Our next stop is Greymouth and a funky café there called Dp:one. Here we get our first chance to stay at a B&B (finally, we won't have to make the kids breakfast). As we arrive at the New River Blue Gums Bed and Breakfast we notice an outside bath; hmm, lovely. We have a great night and a great breakfast before visiting Dp:one, one of the few cafés that has free fluffies.

# DP:ONE CAFÉ

**104 Mawhera Quay
GREYMOUTH**

**C4**

Dp:one Café is established in a way no other business can lay claim to in Greymouth. The name is derived from the words 'deposit plan 1', which indicate that this building is on the first business site in Greymouth. The original building was only one storey and the upstairs was added at a later date.

The café itself has been in the building since 1999 — initially as a rafting base that served coffee and the odd cake. Current owner Alison Sohier has been on site since 2008, originally with one daughter and now with her other daughter Sarah Burdon. Alison does the baking and the books while Sarah and her very small team take care of the rest. The café has evolved into a music spot, with gigs taking place as the mood and opportunity arise. Sarah is a chef and has increased the variety of food available with most things being made to order.

**Dp:one is an eclectic mix of local art, music and people. The West Coast has a particular vibe which seems to be alive and well in the café.** The local crowd patronise it in their droves over the winter months and tend to leave it to the visitors in summer. That said, we arrive in summer and feel very much an extended family vibe as workers and customers move across the boundary of counter that usually exists in a café.

Don't expect a slick-city café, or you will be disappointed. What you *will* find are good hearts, coffee and food wrapped up in West Coast determination to be who you are, not who others think you should be.

Sarah and Alison have plans to use the rented site next door for a local market and are also working towards becoming licensed. We have a feeling that what evolves is guaranteed to be original.

There is a town on the West Coast of the South Island called Pukekura, which by Niki's reckoning means hill school. This would be apt, as there is a lot of learning to be had in this town with an official population of two. The centre of town has two main buildings — the Bushman Centre, including a museum and a café, and the Puke Pub across the road. When we arrive in town the owners of both, Pete and Justine, are heading off in a helicopter to attend an important coastal happening. So we get to speak with Justine's daughter Katie who is able to run the show on her own. Just be careful of the sandflies when you enter.

# BUSHMAN'S CENTRE CAFÉ

**Pukekura**
**LAKE IANTHE, SOUTH WESTLAND**

### L'AFFARE

Pete originally created the Bushman's Centre in Harihari as a shop and museum next to the tearooms. Now located in Pukekura, it has become a major tourist stop on the wild West Coast. Wild is the name of the game here; no beef or chicken is served and where possible the food served is wild. The possum pies are legendary. Pete is the trapper and Katie chief in charge of possum plucking. It is illegal to sell possum meat in New Zealand so you can make a donation to eradicating the pest and in return you can eat a pie, a system that works for all.

This is not a place where you'll receive the perfect flat white — the coffee isn't made on an espresso machine. The sheer number of customers in relation to those doing the work makes an espresso machine impractical, and we think that, in keeping with Coasters' practical character, the easiest way to get the caffeine in takes precedence over any current city trend.

Katie is a real trooper. She bakes, serves, cleans, organises and helps out her parents when she can. During the summer months she crosses the road at around 3 pm and opens the pub. Sometimes backpackers stay instead of passing through, temporarily joining the family and lessening the workload. At one stage there were 11 people running the show; and it is because of hard work and efficiency that the number has reduced, rather than fewer customers coming through the door.

Our kids love the museum, particularly one bit where Niki ended up with water all over her face. Museums have been a bit of a joke on the way around as the kids feel their natural response should be 'Noooo!' But when they have

visited the small-town variety, they have really enjoyed them.

The Bushman's Centre and Café is a must-see if you are in the area. **Go with an open mind and suspend expectation around what makes a café.** Take some time to interact with the townsfolk, and you may find that piece inside that appreciates and maybe even longs for a life less peopled, where being who you are is enough.

Leaving Pukekura and feeling all westie we make the drive to Franz Josef in the rain — not that uncommon on the West Coast. The kids are excited to see a glacier first hand, and in their enthusiasm decide to have a shower in a small waterfall on the way. Yes, shivering *is* a consequence of bathing in freezing cold water.

Next morning we start the long drive to Queenstown. We haven't had any recommendations for cafés on the way, so when we stop to refuel and find another character café, we enjoy the experience of finding New Zealand's best petrol station café. Makarora, at the head of Lake Wanaka, is arguably not the middle of nowhere but it is relatively remote and a welcome respite when the food, fuel, sleep or coffee tanks are getting close to empty.

# MAKARORA COUNTRY CAFÉ, BAR, FUEL, CAMP

**State Highway 6**
**WANAKA–HAAST**

### JUNGLE

In May 2004 David and Sue Howe took over this business and, as happens, added another layer of personality to an already existing presence. They were not involved in cafés before embarking on this project. After 30 years in their respective former careers they felt it was time for a change and to spend some time together. The building was originally a petrol station, and then a small café was added. **Over time and owners it has evolved into its current embodiment — a larger café, gift shop, bar, campground and one of New Zealand's few independently owned petrol stations.** Here you can buy your fishing licence or have a few drinks with the locals on a Friday night.

With the diversity of services available, it is not surprising that the Howes have a staffing philosophy that expects all staff members, including themselves, to be able to do all things, from making the coffee to pumping the petrol. David tends to be the man behind the espresso machine and he brings the precision of his former life as an air-traffic controller to the serious art of making coffee.

This area has always been transient: Maori used the route to access the

## MAKARORA COUNTRY CAFÉ'S **FIVE CUP LOAF**

1 cup self-raising flour
1 cup bran
1 cup milk
1 cup brown sugar
1 cup mixed chopped dried fruit and nuts combined

Preheat oven to 160°C. Line a loaf tin with baking paper. Mix all ingredients together in a large bowl. Pour mixture into the loaf tin and bake for 30–40 minutes. This recipe freezes well.

rich resource of West Coast pounamu, while Pakeha made use of what became a well-known pathway to the gold that was on both sides of the Haast Pass. The variety of visitors making their way to or from the coast continues, with the richness of scenery and experience now being the main focus. There is a collection of number plates from all over the world on one wall of the café.

A mix of tourist supplies and Kiwi culture is available here; we have an inkling that tucked away in a corner somewhere, will be exactly what you need.

Queenstown and Arrowtown are like coming home for Niki. She lived here for a number of years, and now we are returning. Staying with old friends Andy and Kirsty, escaping from the car and taking some time out in this beautiful area is a must. The beauty of lifelong friends is that they go out of their way to help and it isn't long before Andy and Kirsty organise things for the kids and whisk us away to Andy's favourite café in Arrowtown — Provisions. A call had gone out and a number of old friends join for a catch up. This historic cottage filled with food treats and coffee fast became a favourite of ours too.

# PROVISIONS

**Romans Cottage, 62 Buckingham Street
ARROWTOWN**

## L'AFFARE

Provisions is a name you may know that relates to central Otago fruit morphing from its original state into fantastic chutneys, jams and the like under the expert watch of creators Jane Shaw and Pauline Murphy. Pauline and Jane met through their husbands, only to discover an amazing connection — they were both born in Malaya, one year apart — not a common thing for Kiwi girls. What they also have in common is a real foodie interest. Seeing all the beautiful fruit in Cromwell leaving the area in its original form they saw an opportunity to add value, and so Provisions the maker of preserves was born.

Not women to tackle life with little steps, Jane and Pauline decided at the same time to drive the creation of a farmers' market in Cromwell. This is now famous in the area for its wonderful fresh produce. Jane and Pauline noticed that baking was a space that hadn't been filled in the market and created their signature item the 'obscenely good sticky bun', so named by *MasterChef* judge Matt Preston. There is a buzz about these buns that comes up whenever Provisions is mentioned, and a race to make sure you don't miss out at the market and the café.

Provisions is located in one of Arrowtown's historic cottages, just past the main drag. Jane and Pauline worked together with the council to complete the renovation and the locals seem very happy with the result. **The café is an extension of what they have been doing with both the market and the produce. All the food has an item of their produce as an ingredient, and the theme of excellence and taste is contained within also; enjoy.**

# KIRSTY'S **ELDERFLOWER CORDIAL**

Our next day in Queenstown is a day off work and Ruby gets the chance to help make elderflower cordial with Kirsty. It tastes so nice that we decide to include the recipe and take a few bottles for the rest of the trip. Healthier than soft drinks, this adds a little dash of refreshing flavour to the boring water bottle.

**20 large elderflower heads**
**zest of 4 lemons then chopped**
**55 g citric acid**
**1 ½ litres water**
**1 kg white sugar**

Steep the elderflower heads in the water with zest, whole chopped lemons and citric acid that has been dissolved in a little extra water. Leave for 48 hours.

Strain the mix through muslin and keep only the liquid. In a large saucepan bring the liquid just to the boil. Add the sugar and remove from the heat, stirring until the sugar is dissolved. Transfer hot cordial into sterilised bottles and seal. This cordial will keep for months if stored in the fridge.

Over the next couple of days we visit local hot spots, such as Motogrill. Queenstown has a quality to its cafés that reflects its international clientele. Our next featured café also has a history that sees it claiming to be housed in the oldest building in Queenstown, Williams Cottage.

# VESTA

**19 Marine Parade
QUEENSTOWN**

### L'AFFARE

Sometimes a woman reaches a certain age or stage of life and needs a change, a big change; something that can feed her soul and become the outward expression of who she is internally. In 2005 Kim Turner was driven to make that change. She gave up teaching and in a moment of madness bought Vesta. Vesta was owned by a local woman with a knack for creating great food spaces. In her moment of madness Kim thought she was buying a design store only and then realised it was also a café. As is often the way with women, Kim adapted well and now the place is very much her own — café and all.

Williams Cottage is a heritage building, essentially in its original state with the wallpaper peeling in layers to reveal the taste of dwellers gone by. The taste of the current dweller is changing and evolving all the time. New items of interest appear regularly and you can find the perfect gift, exclusive piece of clothing, book or special gem by exploring the little rooms that seem to keep on coming.

**The garden is one of Kim's passions and the glasshouse is her addition. It's set at the lakeside of the property and you can comfortably stay warm, sipping your coffee and watching the world go by.**

One of the things Kim likes about her location is that she is a little off the beaten track of the main shopping area. Tourists who find her are pleasantly surprised and locals head to Vesta for a restful moment away from the throng. There are a number of people that Kim believes just come in to soak up the experience with no intention of drinking, eating or buying. However, when they get through the door they are tempted and often do all three.

Vesta does not have a huge selection of food; the teeny kitchen doesn't allow for it. But what is on offer is tasty and treat-y, the coffee is great, and for a time of respite and exploration send the kids to the park nearby and settle in . . . bliss.

**WILLIAMS COTTAGE**
Queenstown's Oldest House (1864)

# vesta
design store + cafe

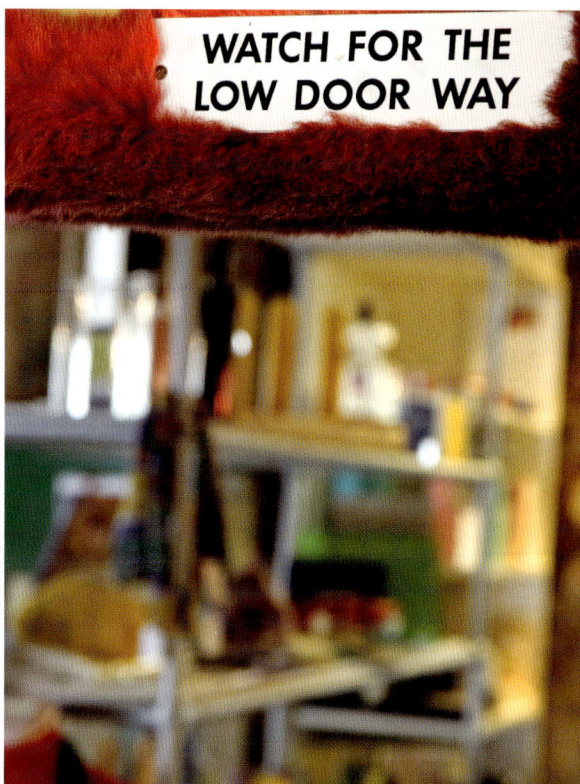

**WATCH FOR THE LOW DOOR WAY**

Our last thing to do in Queenstown is the Glenorchy experience. This starts with a long and winding drive and breathtaking scenery towards Glenorchy. We arrive early and are fitted with wetsuits and lifejackets before boarding a jetboat — these are fast and you get wet. We head up river and are not disappointed. Returning by inflatable kayak is sublime — the scenery, colour, everything. By the end of a long day, the Glenorchy café is a welcome place to relax.

# THE GLENORCHY CAFÉ

**Mull Street**
**GLENORCHY**

### ROASTED ADDIQTION

Ending up in Glenorchy, more particularly at the café, has been a long and winding road for current owner Grant Treleaven. Grant, who is a chef by trade, left his home country of Australia at 21 and set off to travel the world following his passion for cooking and skiing. He got as far as Austria and became a local there over a 15-year stint.

At the end of 2000 he arrived in Queenstown and worked for a time in local restaurants before purchasing an acre of land at Moke Lake, between Glenorchy and Queenstown. Grant seems able to put his hand to most things. He designed and helped build his own home as both project manager and labourer before taking on a job as a completely inexperienced digger driver. The digger pulled him back into the kitchen.

Grant's first sight of the café came when he was employed to do some digging work to sort out its dodgy septic tank. The old Post Office building and style of the café appealed at the time, but it was not for sale. Through a complex chain of events the café eventually came on the market; Grant bought it and has never looked back.

The Glenorchy café is closed for about six weeks in May/June and opens again in conjunction with the Queenstown winter festival, much to the joy of the locals who love the coffee and food. The locals play a part in the café by supplying watercress, eggs, parsley and other items from individuals' gardens, often as a swap for café fare.

**New Zealand reggae/dub live music and pizza play a big part in the café and there are often sounds to enjoy as you soak up Glenorchy.**

GLENORCHY CAFE

With saddened hearts we leave Queenstown. We have loved, shared and enjoyed our time so much that we vow to seriously consider moving here. We leave via Cromwell and stop at the Grain and Seed Café, which is great. We are not really enjoying being back on the road again, however, and the weather is overcast. The kids can feel the dread of doing another café. Yet these are the times when something special turns up, and The Packhouse in Roxburgh is no exception.

# THE PACKHOUSE

**Coal Creek**
**RD1 ROXBURGH**

### L'AFFARE

**Picking cherries warm from the sun and watching your fingers stain as one after another bursts with flavour on your tongue is one reason to always have hope.** In a world that can be challenging, moments like this one hold the good stuff. Maybe a little deep for cherry picking, but Niki has this memory from childhood and was determined to pass it on to our kids. Luckily The Packhouse was recommended by Queenstown locals as a must-do café and this area is well known for its cherries.

Richard and Kerry Groters did the deal of their lives in 2005 when they swapped a three-bedroom unit in Queenstown for a four-bedroom house, 20 acres and The Packhouse, complete with cherries, apricots, nectarines, peaches, greengages, strawberries, raspberries and boysenberries growing in abundance — fruit heaven.

What sold them on the deal was the feeling they got as they sat in the packing shed itself. At the time it was a small arts and crafts shop, but they felt more connected to the history of the building and surrounding orchard. Joseph Tamblyn had imported the first apricots into New Zealand in 1868 and planted them here. The packing house — a mud and stone building — was just that, a shed for packing the fruit.

Today The Packhouse fills many roles. There has been an extension of the arts and crafts that existed to the café and a mini fun park for the kids. Kerry and Richard make their own jams and preserves from the produce that they lovingly tend, and the real-fruit ice cream is very popular with our lot. In fact this café is very popular with all the family. The kids bounce and play mini golf, chat to Peck-a-Toe the parrot and eat fantastic pizza and ice cream.

Niki's dream of introducing them to cherries fresh from the tree is realised. The cherries are not quite ready for 'pick your own', with most of the orchards suggesting the following week would be best. But Richard takes the family into his orchard, finds the ripest tree and lets us go for it . . . Yay.

Should you make your way to The Packhouse you may find Richard waiting the outdoor tables in his gumboots. You may get to sample the fabulous produce and we are pretty sure you'll enjoy the experience as we did. If you do, have a cherry, and think of us.

The rest of the drive to Invercargill reminds us of how rugged our countryside can be, and the further south you go the more rugged it is. By the time we arrive in Invercargill the weather has turned pretty bleak, but the rainbow on our arrival gives some colour over the otherwise grey afternoon. Matthew has heard of a café that is only open on Sundays, and then only for a few hours — it sounds intriguing. On a boys' only drive Ethan and Matthew decide to find the elusive Sticky Beak. Having two guys in a car means, of course, that they can't ask for directions and it's not long before they are lost. It is only by accident that they find Sticky Beak. Sure enough the sign says only Sundays. Bugger, they aren't going to be here long enough. Again, serendipity pays a visit and a woman drives up and greets them. It is Heather, the owner. She has just come back from Bluff and is thrilled to be able to show them around. Sometimes taking the wrong turn is the best thing you can do.

# STICKY BEAK CAFÉ

**62 Vyner Road, Otatara**
**INVERCARGILL**

**BRAVO FROM DUNEDIN**

Owner Heather is an artist, whether she's preparing food or making wire bowls and ornaments. She cooks for the seasons with you in mind, and you never know what is going to be on the menu. The coffee is the filter type, which Heather refers to as hillbilly coffee.

She has been here for over 30 years and mostly her place is used for private bookings — maybe a wedding, or a kids' party where she is Bad Apple, the good witch. **This is a place that is only open on Sunday for a few hours, at least if it's not already fully booked.**

As we wander around the rooms and the gardens outside, amid the herbs and flowers, Ethan and Heather bond in that special way that kindred spirits do. We wish we had time to come back and try Heather's crazy cooking, but that is something you will have to do for us.

On our way out of Invercargill we have to make a stop in Riverton. We have been told of a café there that we can't miss. Of course this is completely the wrong direction — we are headed to the Catlins — yet we are far enough into our trip that we have learnt to trust the bush telegraph and take a leisurely drive to Mrs Clark's Café.

The Sticky Beak
CAFE
Otatara's Original Cafe

# MRS CLARK'S CAFÉ

**108 Palmerston Street**
**RIVERTON**

## HAVANA

Whirlwind is the perfect way to describe the café and personality style of Cazna Gilder. She and husband Pat own and operate this business and they put their hearts and souls into making it the fantastic find of the south.

Pat at one point ran the iconic (sadly now derelict) Arthurs Point Tavern, and this is Cazna's first business venture. They met in Queenstown, and early on in their courting came down to introduce Pat to Cazna's parents. Unable to buy anything in a café before 10 am and finding the building already set up, they made the quick decision to set up themselves. Pat already had an espresso machine and a till, and this rendition of Mrs Clark's was born. Two weeks after the business opened Cazna and Pat got married in the building and they have, pretty much, been there ever since — living upstairs and working down.

**It has taken three years of seven-day-a-week hard graft to turn this into the café it is today with great food, coffee and ambience.** Pat is a chef, originally from Wellington, and Cazna is from Winton and does most of the baking. The muffins that we are lucky enough to get the recipe for are her creation; you must make them or go and try them on site . . . yummy.

They believe food should be fresh, homemade, wholesome, healthy and reasonably priced. The building and staff are family friendly and are happy to cater for kids. Being involved in the local community is also important to this couple. Cazna reckons that what you give out you absolutely receive. The locals support the business with their trade but also with dropping off produce, interesting crockery and anything else they think the young couple may make use of.

You will always find Cazna or Pat in the café; their commitment levels are high. The café is open every day (apart from Christmas), which is a blessing for the coffee fiend and a big ask of self on their part. Riverton has a slow pace, with the Sunday papers arriving on Monday and some produce hard to source, but if you want to watch someone else go at speed while you enjoy the peace, pop in to Mrs Clark's.

## MRS CLARK'S **LEMON DELICIOUS MUFFINS**

2 ½ cups flour
2 teaspoons baking powder
1 cup caster sugar

2 teaspoons lime marmalade
juice and zest of 2 lemons
1 cup natural yoghurt

100 g melted butter
1 ½–2 cups milk

1 ½ cups lemon curd
250 g cream cheese

Preheat oven to 180°C. Line muffin tins. Sift dry ingredients together in a large bowl. In a separate bowl mix the marmalade, lemon juice and zest, yoghurt, melted butter and milk. Make a well in the dry ingredients and pour in the wet mix.

Using a spatula gently mix until just combined; use a light hand. Divide the mix between the muffin cases and squish a teaspoon of lemon curd into the centre of each muffin.

Gently poke a teaspoon of cream cheese into the top of each muffin. Bake for 25 minutes.

It's back the other way and we're finally on our way to the Catlins — more for a break on the way to Dunedin than anything else. We have heard of a place in the middle of nowhere, which we find but they are booked out, so with the kids hungry we have to backtrack to Wyndham for local dairy/takeaway food. But, wait a minute — the sign says café as well. We enter to see the smallest espresso machine we have seen used commercially and learn of a town's tale.

# LEES DAIRY AND CAFÉ

**29 Balaclava Street**
**WYNDHAM**

Gordon and Betty Lee own this dairy, café and DVD store, where you can get a coffee made with an espresso machine and food of the classic takeaway variety. Gordon was born and went to school in Wyndham; a more local man you could not get. He has ties to Ngai Tahu that he is not quite sure of, but tangata whenua is a title that fits. Gordon laughs because most strangers who come into the dairy are expecting a Chinese face behind the counter and are surprised to find him or Betty.

Fifteen years ago Betty and Gordon renovated an empty space and created the business. They are open from 6 am to 8 pm, seven days a week, and are only closed on Christmas day afternoon. They have seen three generations of staff go through the business in their time, and being so local are able to discern which teens are going to be the right ones to employ.

**If you listen to Gordon for long, you'll feel like moving to Wyndham in a heartbeat. It's the best place in the world, he reckons, with sports facilities and three trout-fishing rivers within walking distance.** There are 700 people in the town with three petrol stations serving a large rural area, and once a year the population swells to 7000 during the Burt Munro Street race — when 52 million dollars worth of bikes come to town. The staff who serve us are great and Gordon strikes a chord with Niki, who could stay and talk for days; but the road beckons.

We stop for the night at Owaka Bay in the Catlins. We haven't planned to do a café here, but it's not long before we get to know the owners. We enjoy good coffee and Southland sushi (a toasted cheese sandwich rolled up), and feel so at home that we decide to include it.

51

# CATLINS CAFÉ

**3 Main Road**
**OWAKA**

**ALLPRESS**

Should you ever want full-on butler service from your local café you need to move to Owaka, or at least to nearby Pounawea. Aileen and Steve Clarke met in the Air Force where Aileen was a publications specialist and Steve a motor mechanic. They went on to travel the world, both training as butlers and working in the likes of manor houses. They eventually made their way back to New Zealand, and on a trip to Aileen's family home came across the café for sale. The building had been empty for two and a half years and the previous owners had started to convert the building to a café but changed their minds. Aileen and Steve stepped into the breech.

The Clarkes arrived in early March 2010 and decided that they wanted a gentle opening, so aimed for the 1st of April thinking the tourist flood would have subsided. That planning wasn't the best, however, as they forgot about Easter, and Good Friday was their second day open. All that was possible was to cope with the crowds with an attitude of 'what you don't know you make up'.

This philosophy has served them in other areas of their business. The fireplace surround is a mish mash of cemetery surround, an old bed head, a tractor gear stick and a couple of bits from an old Singer sewing machine. The cheese boards are all made from recycled local kauri. When we arrive they are about to embark on an outdoor area with raised garden beds using recycled sleepers from a local farmer's swamp.

As is often the case in small-town cafés, using local produce is really important. These guys make use of local beef and blue cod along with the legendary Greenway Gourmet Pies. **The Clarkes' philosophy is to provide somewhere you can eat well without having to have chips on your plate; although if you must, they are available.** Fresh, homemade food that reminds you of when you were a kid is the direction the Catlins Café takes.

Catlins Café is open seven days a week from breakfast through to dinner. The locals are regulars, as are the huge numbers of national and international tourists who come into the area.

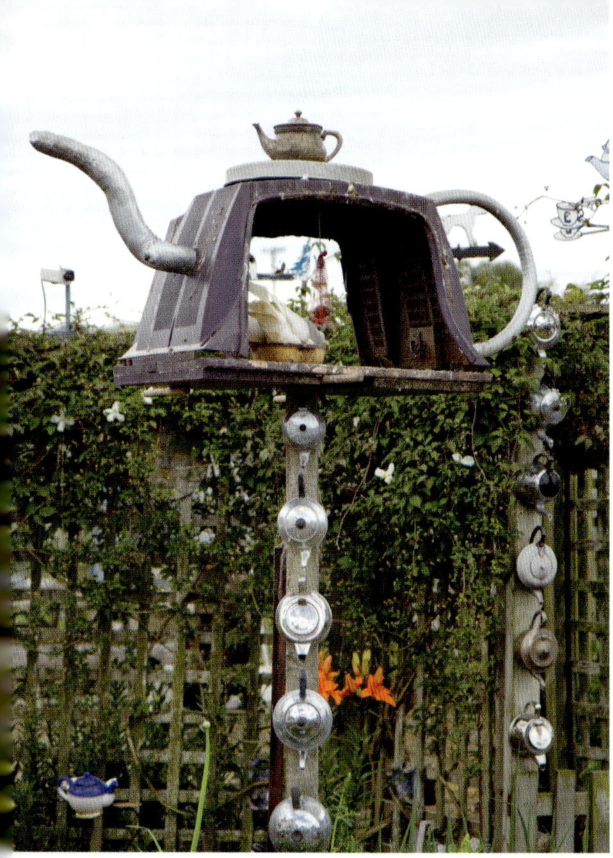
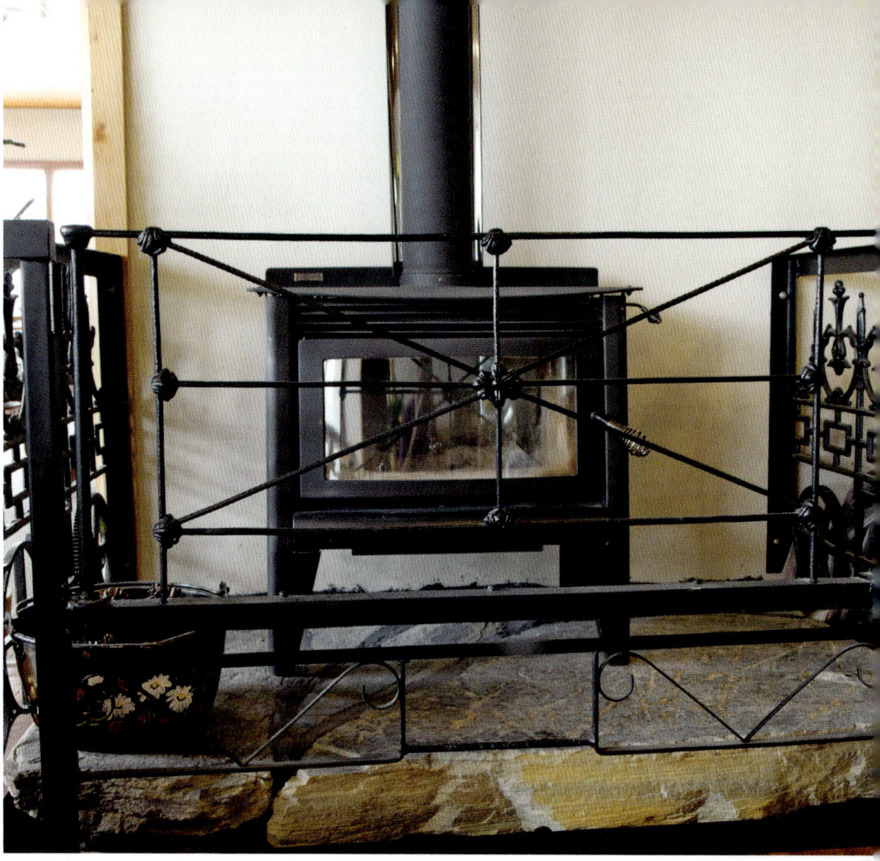
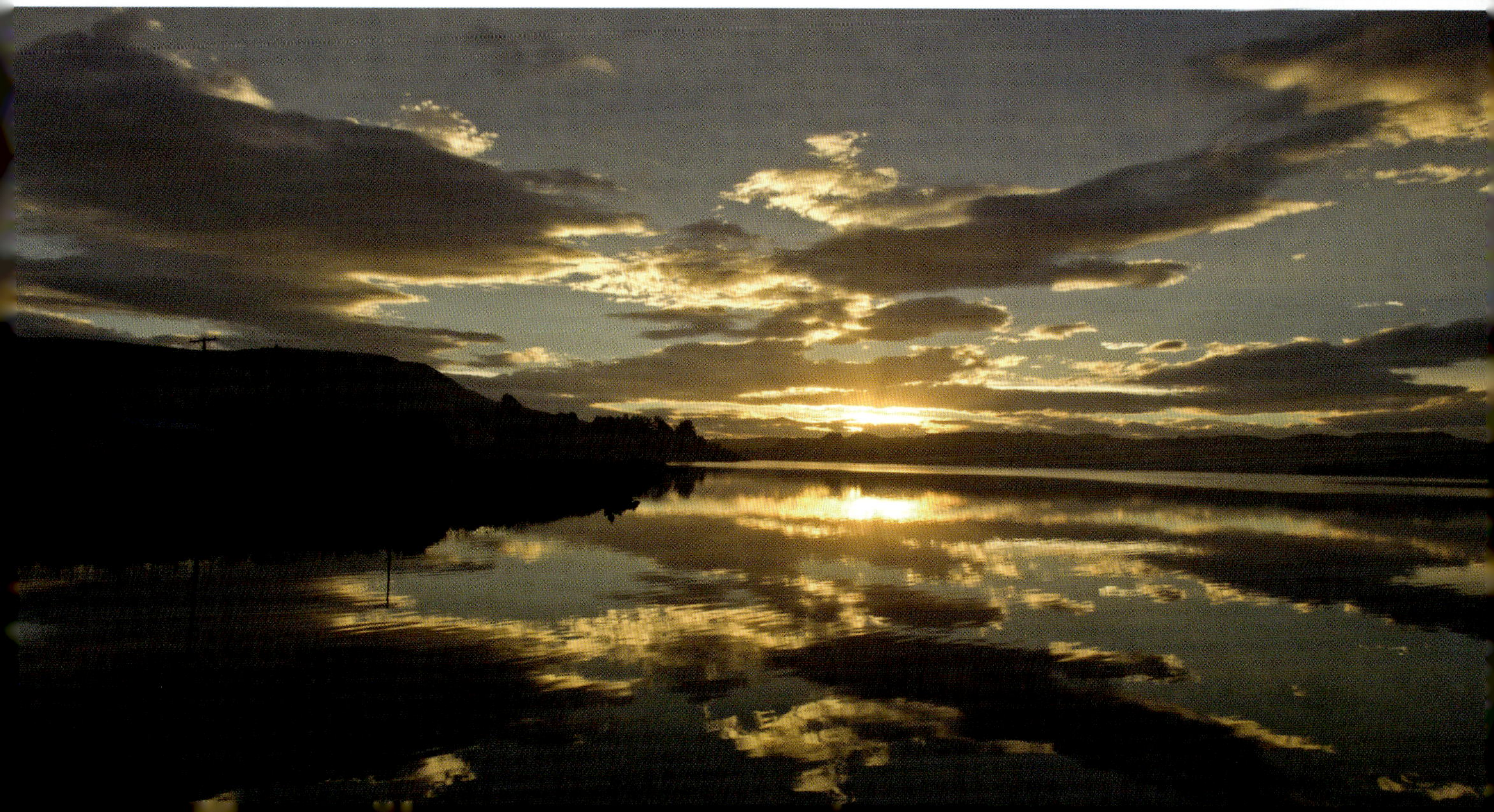

Dunedin is a major city and the country's most southern. As we arrive, we've forgotten how large a city can be. It's not anywhere as big as Auckland, but nevertheless a city with more than a few good cafés. We spend a few days here, visiting those that have been recommended and some that aren't. The Starfish Café in St Clair is a lovely spot by the beach, or try the Circadian Rhythm Café just down from the Octagon for great vegan food. However, as is our tradition, we choose something a little different, and Chucky's provides just that.

# CHUCKY'S COFFEE HOUSE

**Stuart Street**
**DUNEDIN**

**OWN ROAST**

It seems apt that, as we are writing the book, locating the street number and phone number for Carlin Lawrence's coffee hallway is not an easy process. Chucky's Coffee House is located just up from the Octagon in the downstairs hallway of Carlin's terrace home. If you didn't know about it you wouldn't be able to go.

Carlin was living here when the music shop a couple of doors down closed. He is a 'muso' himself as well as a projectionist and actor. **As the lost record seekers passed by his doorway Carlin decided to make them a coffee, and so a business began.**

To be free is a philosophy that Carlin seems to live by. The coffee house closes at two — originally that was so he could go surfing, but he has lost his wetsuit. His varied career choices allow a certain freedom and by having coffee in the hallway he is able to change the blend daily if he likes; he does like and his customers do like, too. Every coffee is three dollars, hot chocolates are two dollars and fluffies are free . . . if you don't mind the absence of marshmallows.

Music is a big part of Carlin's existence, with albums changing hands in the hallway and gigs taking place on the front steps, which are not enormous. The odd poker game has been known to go down and you get points if you can locate the chips.

Food at Chucky's is random in nature — ranging from none to whatever takes his fancy on the day. So the food is random and the blend of coffee changes, but you can be sure the coffee you get will be consistently good and that Carlin Lawrence will live his life to the full.

CHUCKYS COFFEE HOUSE

If you're wondering whether Dunedin has any more-traditional cafés, then the next one could be your cup of tea — so to speak.

# STRICTLY COFFEE COMPANY

**23 Bath Street**
**DUNEDIN 9014**

### STRICTLY COFFEE COMPANY

Strictly Coffee Company is owned by self-confessed 'Johnny-come-lately' Duncan Northover and his partner Lesley Keen. The business has been in operation since the late 1990s and Duncan and Lesley took ownership around 2005. They may be relatively new to this café but they have a history in hospitality and have had instruction from Kiwi roasting guru Craig Miller about the best way to roast coffee.

Strictly has always been a roastery and the focus is coffee not food. That said, the quality of food on offer is often above the standard café fare. Lesley is a kitchen fiend and all the food is made on the premises, apart from the bread.

**Strictly is very much like the Tardis (Doctor Who's time-travel machine) in that from the outside it looks tiny but once inside it is positively spacious.** The building is approximately 110 years old and a former stamp-maker's premises where they could look out the long window over what was at the time paddocks, while they worked. The building has evolved over time to a solid piece of contemporary history in the making.

There are some rules Duncan and Lesley stick to which would serve every aspiring café owner well:
- No excuse for bad coffee.
- Always hire nice staff who leave their attitude at the door. (NB: Prudence the fantastic manager.)
- Remember to have fun.

Ninety per cent of Strictly customers are local return business that comes through the door every day of the week. The rest have either stumbled off course, been drawn in by spiffy reviews, or are aficionados from out of town, like us. This is a community café in the heart of the city, with great coffee.

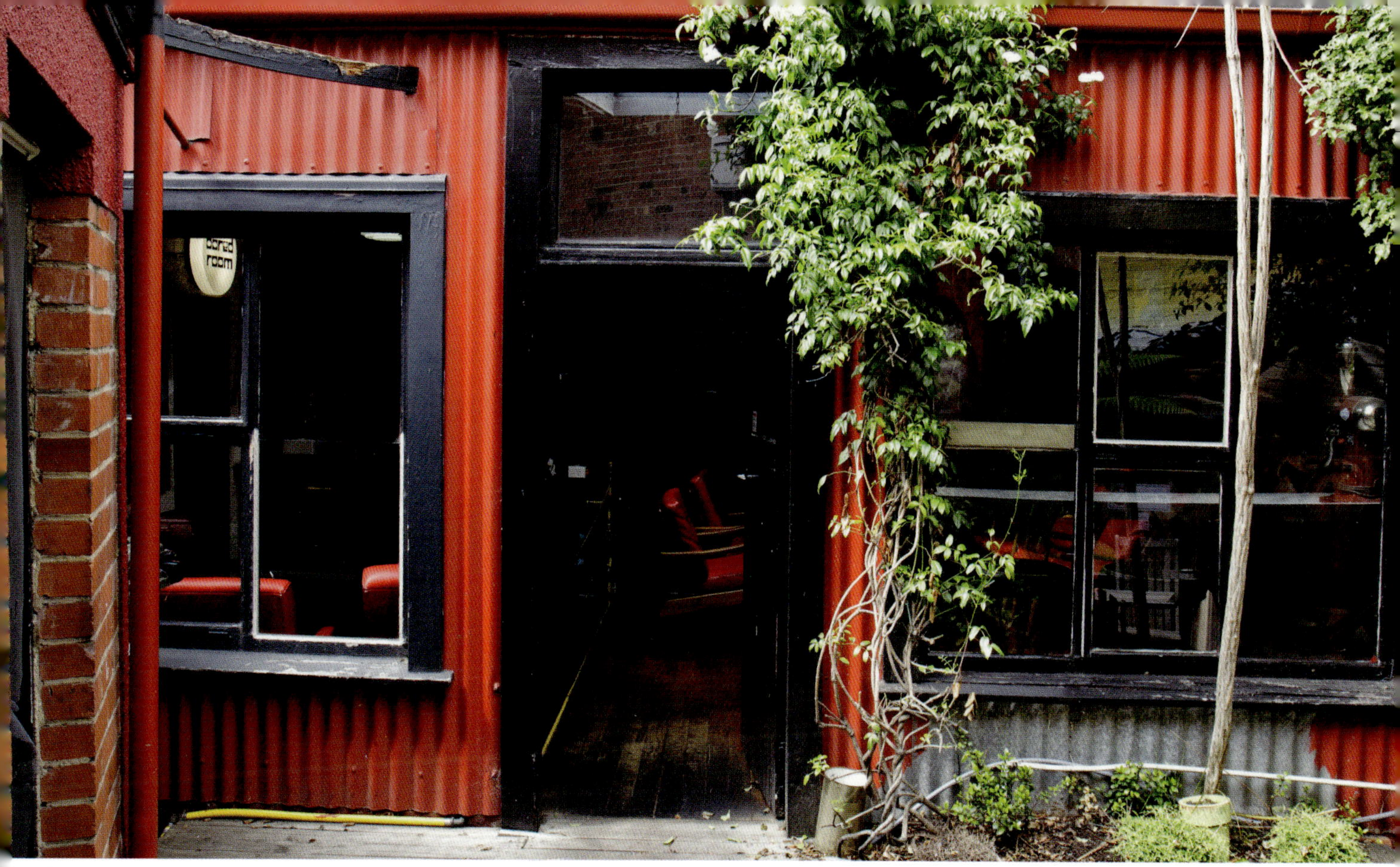

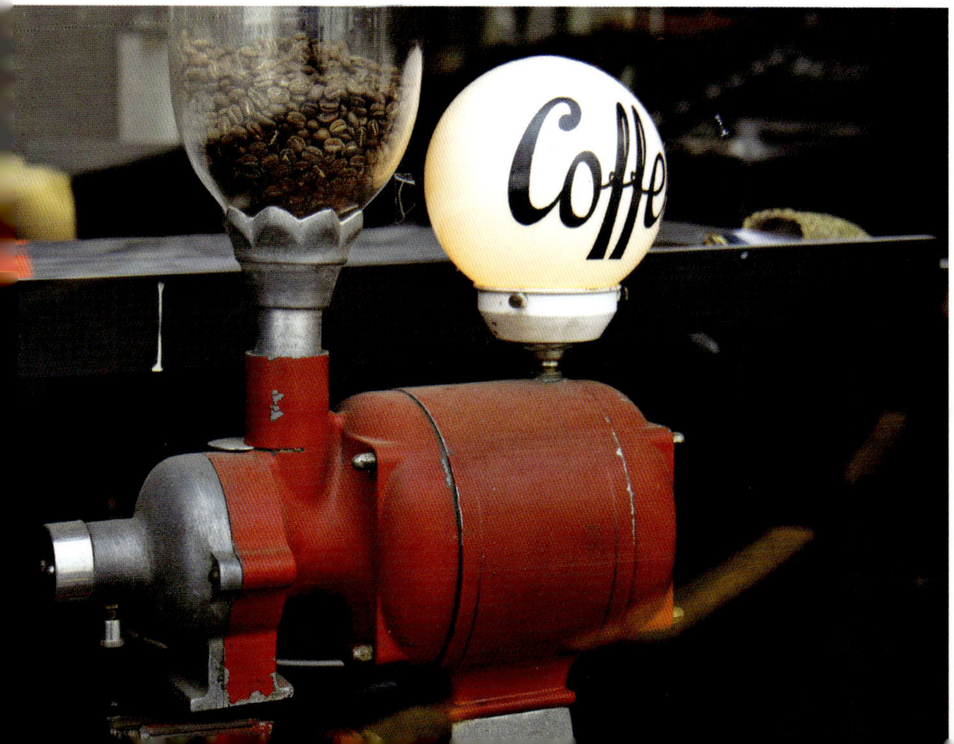
Coffe

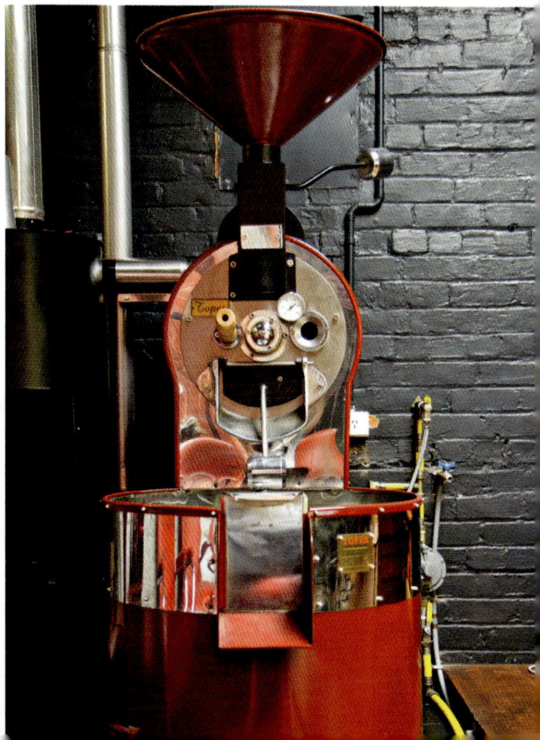

# HISTORY OF COFFEE

In the late 19th century a gentlemen might retire to have a few puffs of his pipe and a coffee, if he didn't like whisky. This, however, was not coffee of the espresso type, but the percolator type. In 1863 a Dunedin restaurant called Riordans had a filter machine called the Parisian Hydrostatic Percolator. It was hailed as producing the finest pure coffee, and you might have your coffee with cream, or even chicory.

In 1822 Frenchman Louis Bernard Rabaut invented a machine that was possibly the first espresso machine; it wasn't until early in the 20th century that they started to gain some popularity. The Italian company Cremonesi made espresso machines in the 1930s that had vertical boilers. The problem with these was they could quite literally blow their tops. There was a hand-pulled lever to create the pressure and push the water through the coffee beans.

In 1946 Milan-born coffee maker Achille Gaggia invented the precursor to the modern espresso machine, whereby the pressure is created by a spring system. The Second World War created a scarcity of coffee, and by the 1950s it was 11 times more expensive than tea in Australia. Although espresso machines were arriving in New Zealand in the 1950s they were few and far between. By the 1960s another Italian company called Faema had devised a pump-driven machine. The difficulty with these machines in New Zealand was getting parts and being able to maintain them. So filter machines ruled in Aotearoa.

By the 1960s the Cona coffee filter machine had firmly established itself as the more cost-effective solution. It could be built and serviced locally, and so the days of Robert Harris and Burton Hollis came into being. Your Cona coffee at a Cobb and Co ruled, and if you wanted luxury you might add Irish whisky and cream and turn it into an Irish coffee. Matthew remembers hangovers from nights on these. The international food company Nestlé revolutionised coffee drinking at home by marketing instant coffee. It became the drink of choice, as you could easily make one during a break for commercials on television. It's a bit different now — you can make a three-course meal, go buy an espresso and still be back before the commercials are over.

and scalding water shot across the café. It wasn't long before they were making great coffee, and along with taking up the roasting challenge, New Zealand's modern espresso café came into being. Although the technology has become more sophisticated, the basic function of an espresso machine hasn't changed.

They still have the primary function of keeping water to just below boiling, and creating pressure to push this water through the ground beans to make an espresso. The early machines were a single head, which could make two cups at once, and now you can get up to four heads. This is where the skill of a properly trained barista

## It wasn't long before they were making great coffee, and along with taking up the roasting challenge, New Zealand's modern espresso café came into being.

So what led to the rise of espresso machines and espresso becoming our preferred choice for drinking coffee? In the 1980s New Zealand changed, import duties came off and we became a more internationally aware country. We travelled more and young men wanting to make a name for themselves began importing espresso machines. Craig Miller — an Auckland coffee stalwart who set up Miller's Coffee — bought his Faema E61 model in the early 1980s and many followed suit. With the passion of these young New Zealand coffee pioneers, they figured out how the machines worked, serviced them — even if sometimes they forgot to turn the water off

comes in. It's easy to show someone how to make an espresso, but try making eight at once, all the right combination of espresso and milk, and maintaining the high quality while serving hundreds of cups of coffee. There are world barista championships each year, and making a great coffee has become an art, one that we in New Zealand are very good at. So you may well be asking, 'Tell me which café uses the most beans?'

Hate to tell you, but it's the Wild Bean cafés . . .

It wouldn't be right to say goodbye to Dunedin without visiting Port Chalmers, where Niki's dad grew up. Port Chalmers has a real sense of history, from the old Chick's Hotel to the shops along the main street. Niki was even able to show us the house her dad grew up in. In the main street, next door to a second-hand clothes shop, is the Port Royale café.

# THE PORT ROYALE CAFÉ

**10 George Street, Port Chalmers**
**DUNEDIN CITY**

## SAVOY BROWN COFFEE COMPANY

Many of us are attempting to become aware of where our food comes from and what we do with our waste — either from a genuine desire to be kinder to the planet and take responsibility for our actions, or because it is the done thing. Café owners Sharon Tisdall and Jeff Edgerton have their feet firmly planted in the first camp. Their ideal is to live off the grid and make the café as self-sufficient as possible.

The Port Royale was around long before Sharon and Jeff came along. They speak of the wonderful legacy they bought into with great food and coffee and a strong local following. The bagels have lasted the change of ownership and the unusual toppings are talked about for miles around in a positive way. Jeff and Sharon added to what was already an unpretentious place that caters to young and old alike. One of the pluses to living in Port Chalmers is the cross-section of society that lives here. This is not a suburb that is easily labelled as any particular social strata; everyone is all in together.

**Roasting the beans that make the wonderful coffee on offer is done by Jeff and is only one of the 'source to table' initiatives they have in the pipeline. Sharon grows vegetables and herbs for the café, with intentions of rearing pigs for pork also.** It's not something you can do in a suburban back yard, so it is lucky they live rurally. Cardboard from the café is used for composting and coffee grinds also go back to the earth. Sharon and Jeff have their own spring on their land, and in time hope to be free of needing externally supplied power.

The giving back does not stop with things of a green nature; witness the support that is given to, and received from, the local art community. Art is exhibited with no commission taken and they have a special relationship with

Jim Cooper the famous ceramic artist; he has a number of his works on display.
Sharon and Jeff have a great take on life, with the goal of keeping things little and fresh, living in a woolshed, keeping horses, planting trees and being involved with the community. Their relationship with others and the earth is all a part of living their simple kind of life.

*As we continue on our road trip, there is more nostalgia. On the long drive to Lake Ohau we pass Oamaru, Niki's birth place. It only takes a moment to pass through so the nostalgia is short-lived. We continue driving for quite a while before arriving at a local airfield and a café we have heard of.*

# KAHU CAFÉ

**Flight Centre, 68 Airport Road
OMARAMA**

We arrive at Kahu Café at the end of a very long day. We don't really want to stop here now, but know that time and money prevents us returning to the area for this café that seems elusive in place and character. A number of friends have given very sketchy directions and very positive comments.

Lana serves us a good coffee and tells us some of the history; she goes on to play a mean game of last card with Ruby, whose tolerance for brothers has worn out. It seems that Mayan started the café, having worked in gliding and realised the potential of the empty former Omarama Gliding Club/office space. She is now in Christchurch. Lana and Dagmar, who worked together on the Hollyford track, managed to meet up again and now run the show, with the help of Woofers.

**All the fare on offer is made from scratch, including the bread. The food and drink is local, simple and genuine, whether it's beer and wine or the locally grown Aoraki Smokehouse Salmon.** The chicken bin, and therefore the chickens, do not do so well from the café as very little goes to waste. The menu changes to make use of what is in the fridge and pantry on the day.

Gliding is one of the big drawcards for this area and, by extension, for the café. Customers often arrive by way of wind and wing; as one who arrived by road, there is a tinge of jealousy. Watching the gliders and the elegant biplane do their thing in the fading light and sublime sunset, while drinking great coffee, is refreshing at the end of the day.

International tourists pass through the area and during the Christmas period a number of intergenerational campers fill the local campground. Kahu Café has been in operation since around 2005 serving breakfast, lunch and dinner. It's done well, with mainstream food given a bit of a twist.

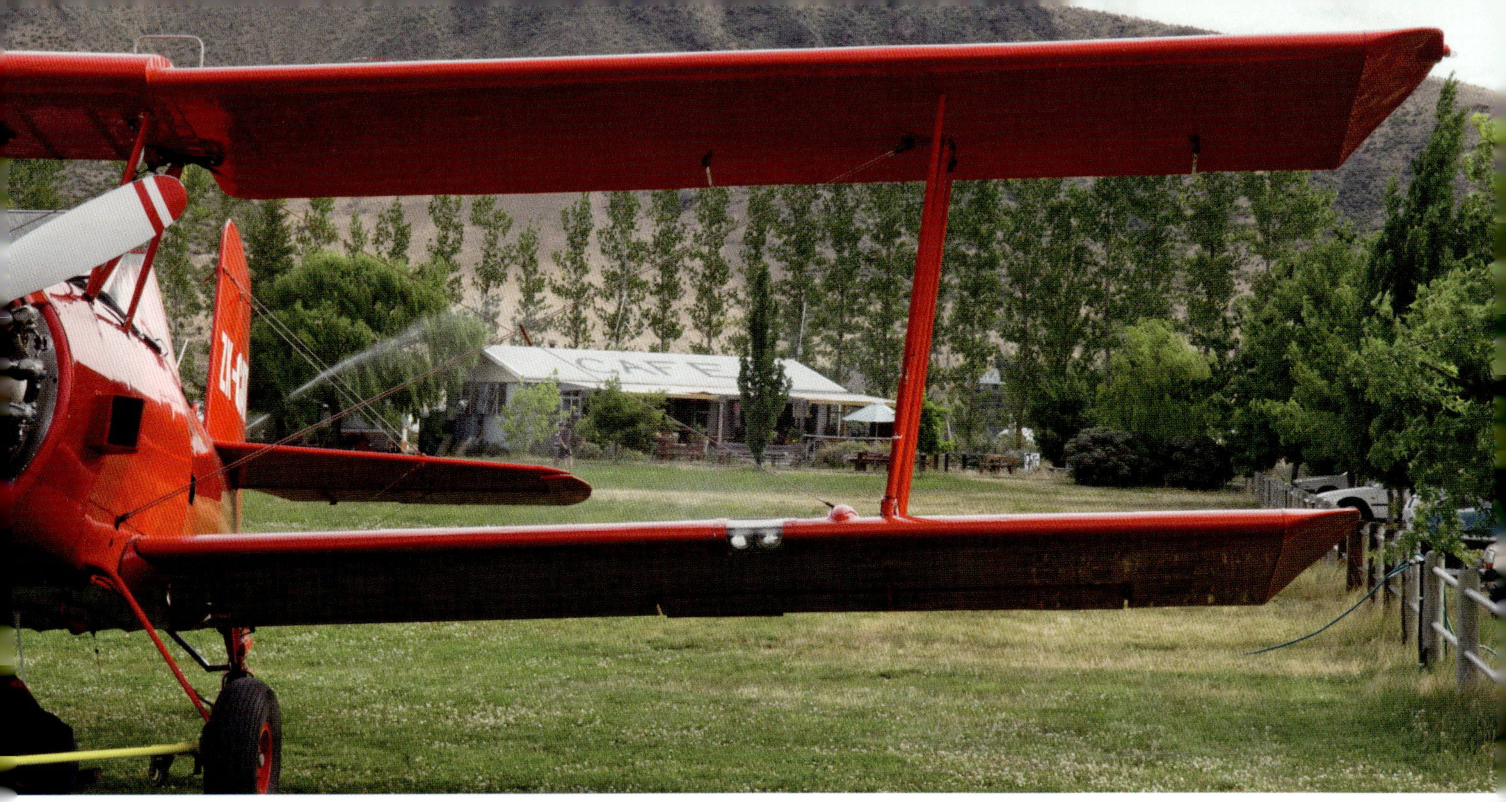
CAFE

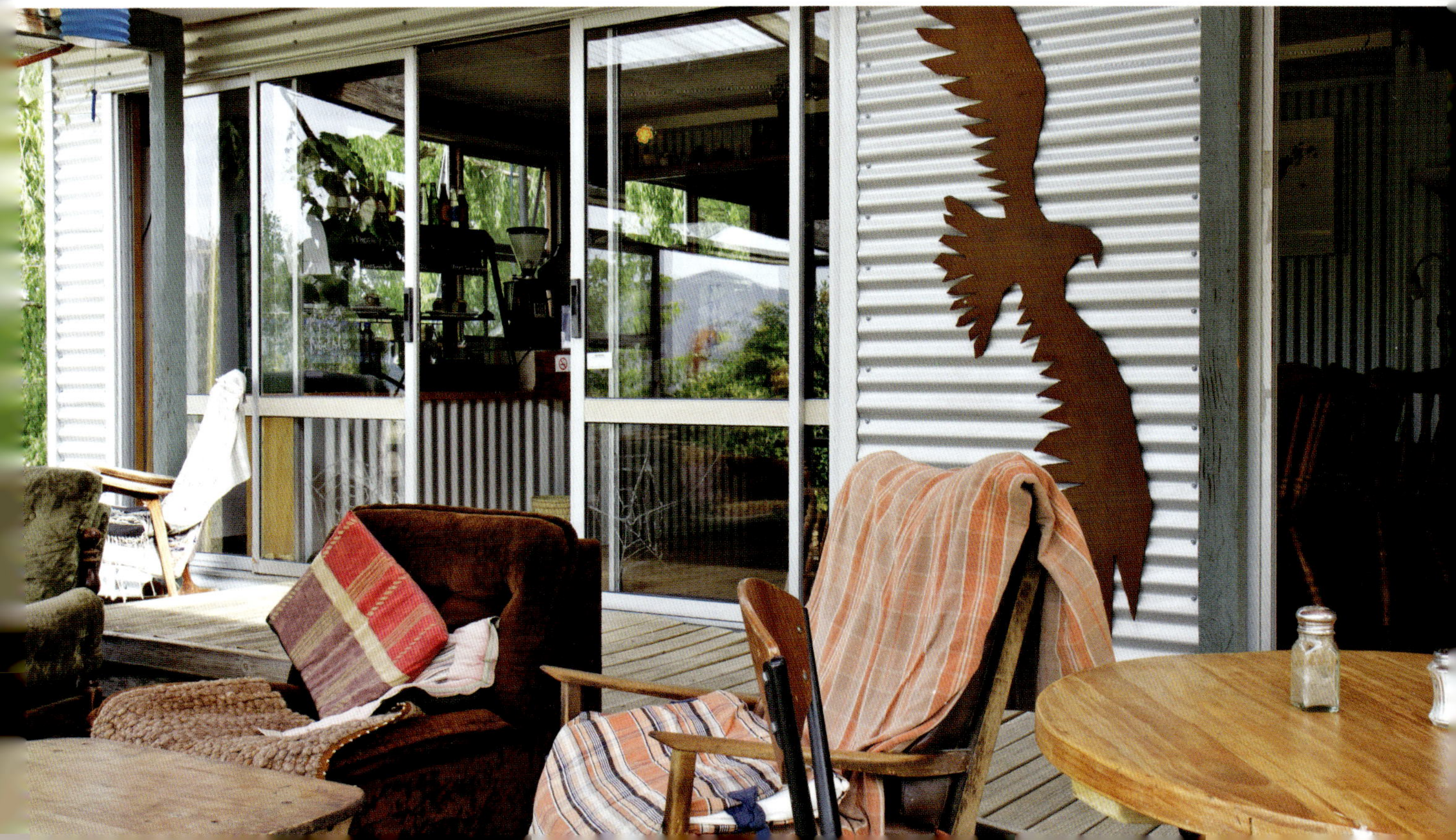

*After two days at the beautiful Ohau lodge, which has great coffee, it's late afternoon before we make it to Timaru. Matthew used to pay flying visits to Timaru when he was in the corporate world. He'd fly in by Cessna, occasionally having a drama with the landing gear not coming down. His memory is of a town with no style or cafés. Of course, that's almost 20 years ago and things have changed.*

# ARTHUR STREET CAFÉ

**8 Arthur Street
TIMARU**

C4

Arthur Street Café really appeals visually. The colours and eclectic set-up of the rooms and outside area give a feeling of ease and yet heightened awareness. It all sounds a bit 'out there', and yet if you go and spend some time there we're sure you will understand what we mean. (It is closed on Sundays.)

Juliette Whitley is the café's owner/operator. Originally a hairdresser, the chemicals became too much for her hands and she moved into the world of coffee. **Coffee has always been the priority here with the food side of the business organised within a week of opening. That said, the food is good.** Herbs and vegetables are grown on site and help provide for the catering company that is now in action.

Music is one of Juliette's passions and she is away at gigs around the country most weekends. There is an extensive album collection tucked away and Saturday is the regular spot for live music at Arthur Street. Being located on the outskirts of the town centre does not seem to be a problem as there are plenty of regulars who call the place home and are often seen three times daily. There is a boardroom that seats 10 upstairs gets good use.

Opened in April 2006, Arthur Street Café has gluten-free retail produce, fantastic coffee, good food, really helpful staff, music just the way we like it, and an atmosphere that soothes the soul.

*Christchurch is where we will spend the next week, and we wonder what we will find. We arrive during a hiatus between earthquakes. Matthew is looking forward to seeing his family, and we wonder how much of the garden city has been disrupted.*

Cafe

We arrive in Christchurch at a traumatic time, only a few months after their first major earthquake in September. Now, of course, things are much sadder, but when we visit in the summer of 2011, New Zealand is just grateful that there was no loss of life. In the week we spend here we feel the aftershocks that Cantabrians are getting used to. After the tragic events of February 2011, we know the city will be changed for ever. This section is a remembrance of some of the character cafés that struggled to make it through the quake. Here you will see them as they were, and meet their owners — Cantabrians who won't let disaster stop them from doing great things.

# LYTTELTON COFFEE COMPANY

**29 London Street**
**LYTTELTON**

## LYTTELTON COFFEE COMPANY

One of the best cafés in the UK with Australasian roots is Flat White, and one of the original partners is Kiwi James Gurnsey. For varying reasons once the business was established he was unable to live in the United Kingdom, so in 2006, at a loose end, James came home and set up what was one of the best cafés in New Zealand — the Lyttelton Coffee Company. He didn't do it alone, however — Stephen Mateer had the lease for the building and they swapped renovating for rent, eventually managing to buy it.

Roasting has been a steep learning curve for the duo. They bought the roaster without much experience and bumbled along via the internet, feeling their way through until they found a professional who helped get them established. Surprisingly, with such shaky beginnings, the coffee is grand.

Many cafés have the support of their community once open, but Lyttelton Coffee Company had locals working for a week for no pay in order to get the place up and running. Opening finally took place in 2007, much to the joy of all involved. The building is mostly red brick and wood, and the diverse items cramming the place keep it earthy and interesting.

**The food is not restaurant food but is of a high quality, with the locals playing their part in supply and demand. A number of produce items are swapped for coffee and breakfast.**

Live music abounds, with musicians turning up off their own bat to play. The music is symbolic of the community nature of this café and roastery; all those who wish to participate do so and collectively we all benefit.

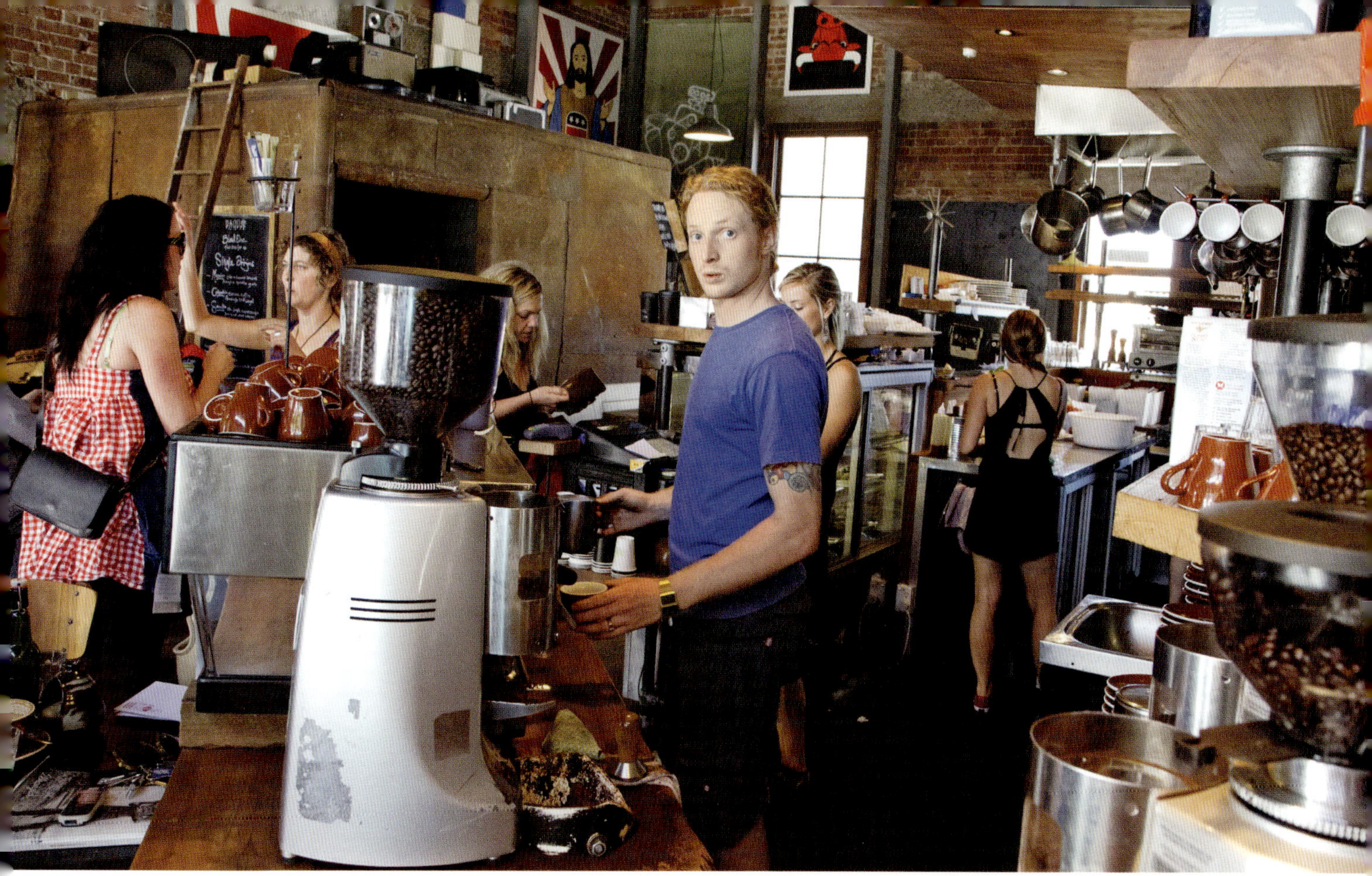

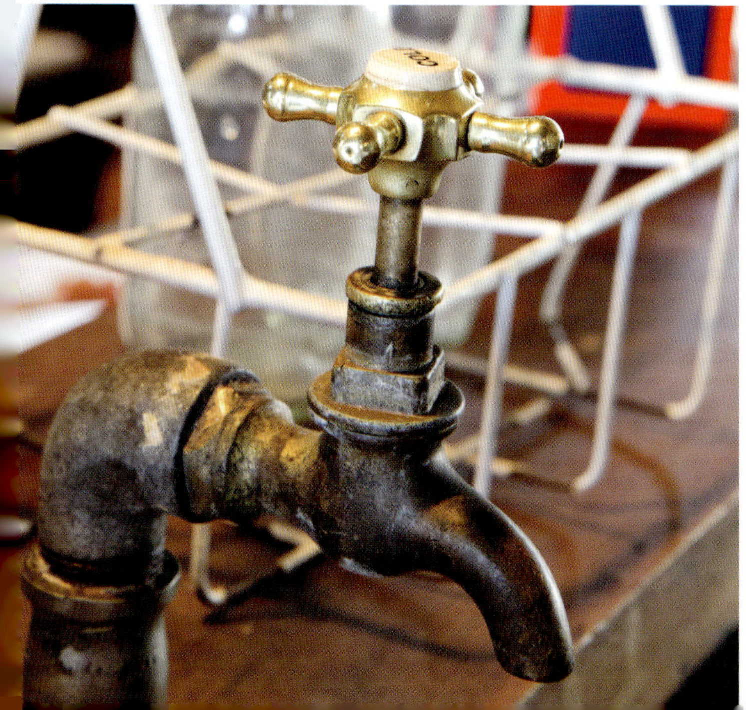

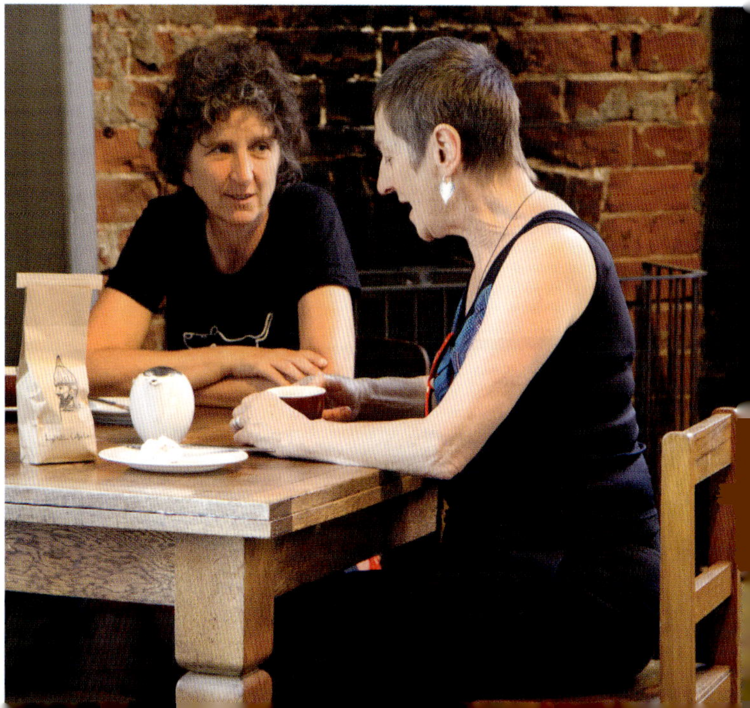

# UNDER THE RED VERANDAH

**502 Worcester Street, Linwood**
**CHRISTCHURCH**

### VIVACE AND QUEEN BEAN

Mandy Heasley is chief in charge at Under the Red Verandah, and has held this position since 2004 when she bought the existing business from Glyn Abbot and Rodger Hickin, who opened it in 1997. Mandy has a lot of good things to say about the founders — one is that they made it possible for her to buy the business, another that she will never be able to fill the shoes of master baker Glyn. We wonder if Mandy is being modest in her self-evaluation, as the baking we saw and tried was fantastic. Mandy is a chef by trade but baking is her passion.

A career in fine arts was the direction Mandy was originally headed until she realised she could use her artistic ability to create food and cafés that people feel comfortable in. She took her first foray into café ownership when she bought an old greasy spoon on High Street and turned it into the Globe Café — a very popular destination for several years. She then moved to Hanmer Springs where she opened and ran the Powerhouse Café, before returning to her home of Christchurch and the UTRV, as it's affectionately known. When she took over the café she wanted to stay close to the original print and renovated only for reasons of size and flow.

One of the biggest assets UTRV has is its staff. **We witness great service under the constant arrival of many customers, and not only that but the ease with which the staff seems to cope is evidence of great systems in place.**

Family is also an integral part of this café, with Mandy and her husband Andy's three children working in the café at times. Mandy's dad is a grower and much of the produce is supplied by him. The community is part of the family, too. When the earthquake struck in 2010 Mandy made coffee from the closed café. She says it gave people somewhere to go to and that's what cafés are about. The second time around, sadly, the old building had to be demolished, but Mandy renovated the small building in the garden to a smaller version, serves coffee and simple takeaway food, and is already planning the rebuild; possibly even a new name — After the Red Verandah.

# UNDER THE RED VERANDAH'S
## BLACKCURRANT JAM

**1 kg blackcurrants**
**2 cups water**
**6 cups sugar**
**1 teaspoon lemon zest**

Remove stalks from blackcurrants. Put all ingredients into a preserving pan. Bring to the boil and boil rapidly for 15 minutes or until setting point is reached. Pour into sterilised jars. Makes about four 350 ml jars.

# C1 ESPRESSO

**150 High Street**
**CHRISTCHURCH 8142**

## C1 ESPRESSO

Sam Crofskey and Fleur Bathurst have owned C1 since 2003. They are professional baristas and Sam says that when they arrived at the café, the coffee culture in Christchurch was such that it was difficult to find a decent barista. Lawyers applied for the positions, going out for breakfast was unusual, and specific types of coffee weren't done.

In 2006 they began to think about how to future-proof the business and stay ahead of the pack. The solution they arrived at was one that would have been hard to guess — they started growing their own organic coffee beans in Samoa in conjunction with an initiative set up there called Women in Business Development. This venture has been wonderful not only for the Samoan farmers who are involved, but for the C1 business. Families on the island, which would have been split up, with some going away to work, are now able to utilise the land around them to support themselves.

The first roast was completed in December 2010 and Sam intends to bring individual farmers from Samoa to see where their produce ends up. Currently Sam and Fleur take a couple of staff with them each time they visit Samoa. It is an eye opener for the staff, as people in Samoa are often living at a financial level that would be unacceptable to the average Kiwi.

**The café itself is the first one off the lips of locals when we are seeking recommendations. C1's reputation is huge and it seems well deserved.** Sam reckons that their staff are one of the major drawcards, with regulars coming from far and wide to just touch base with the people. By 2010 the café seated 250. The great thing is that it is set up in a way that you are in your own nook or cranny, unaware of the size of the place.

Plans are constantly afoot, with honey, juice and chocolate sauce being added to the current Samoa connection. The interior of the café is ever-changing with local art being displayed and Fine Arts students creating posters that symbolise the café annually.

C1 is an institution, and the fact that the building was destroyed won't stop them from keeping the tradition alive.

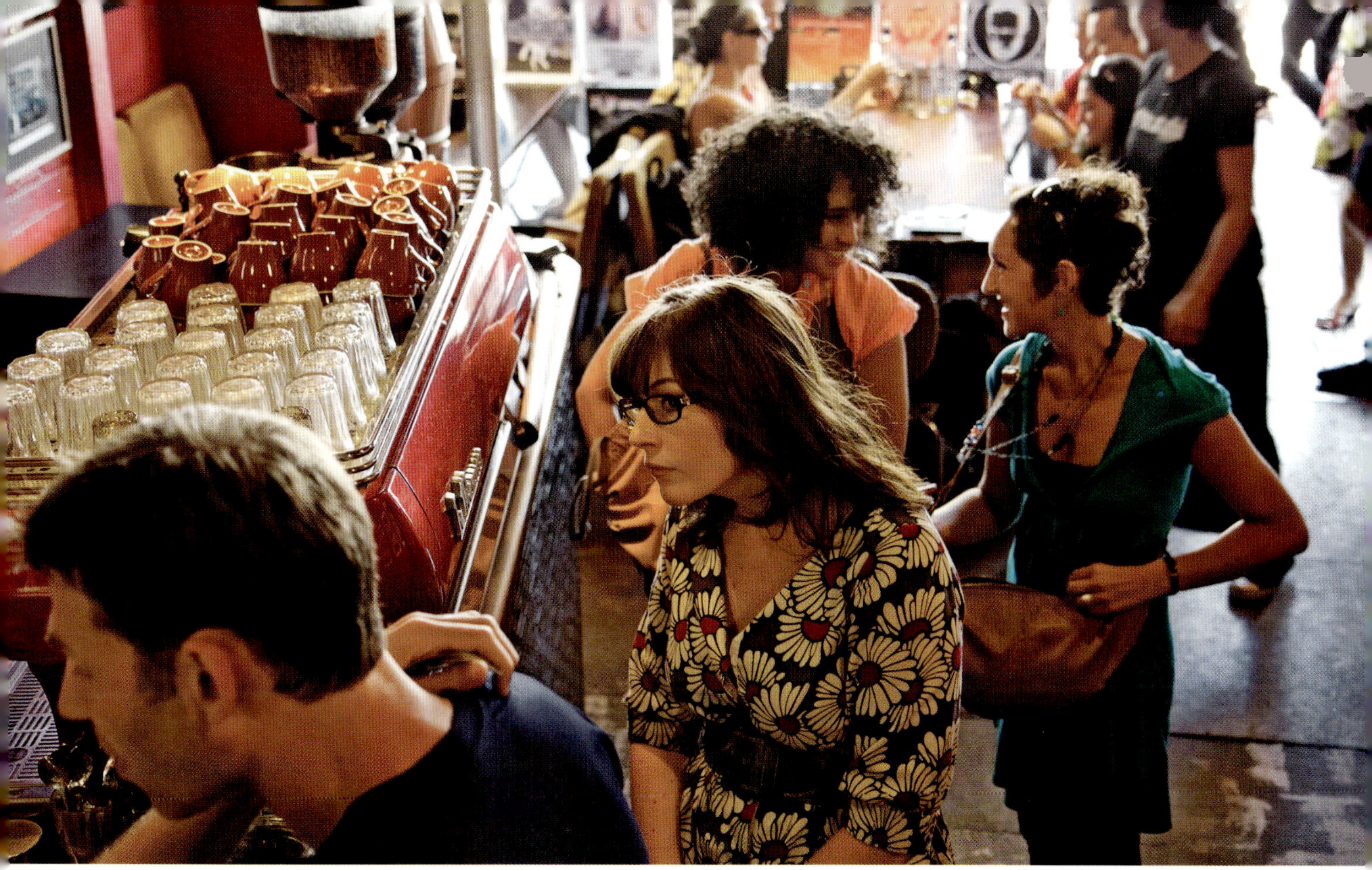
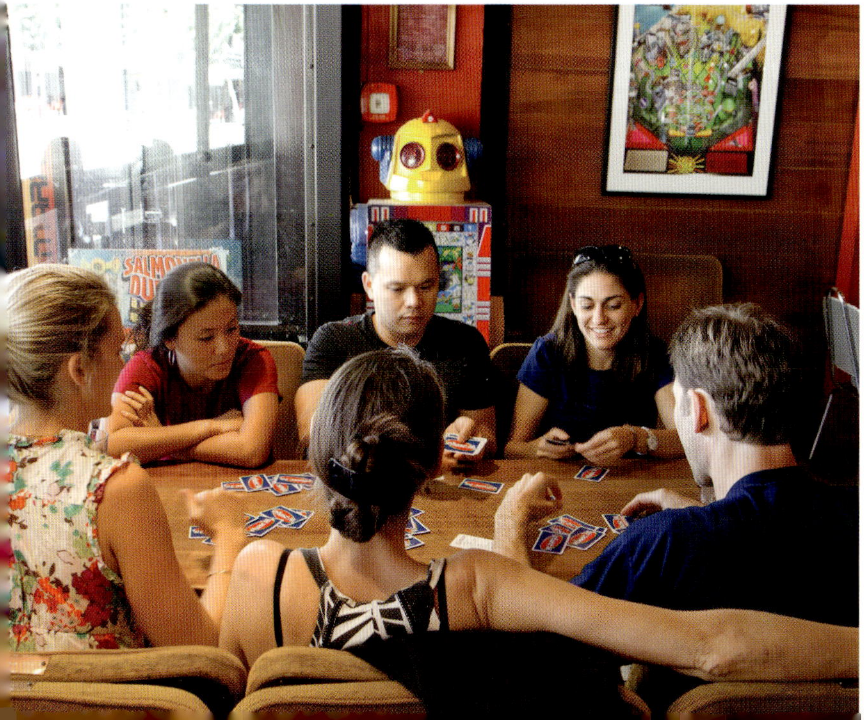
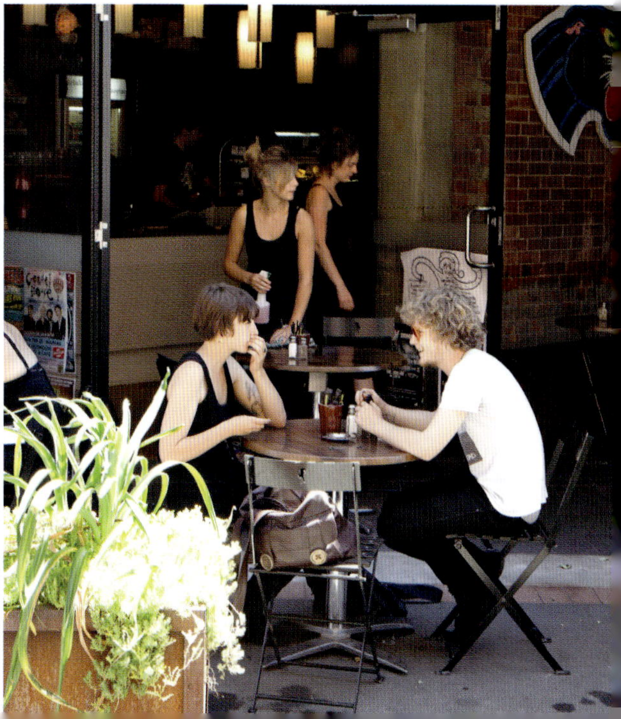

Once you get out of Christchurch city the devastation seems to disappear, but some suburbs are worse hit than others. The Addington Coffee Co-op in Addington was lucky and survived both quakes. Rhombus Café and Roastery in Heathcote was not so lucky. We hope they will be back up and running, as Matthew loves their smoothies.

While we were in Christchurch, Matthew and his brother Ben, visiting from Australia, decided to take a drive to Methven in search of a café, via the Dunsandel Store.

# DUNSANDEL STORE

**Main South Road
DUNSANDEL**

## HUMMINGBIRD

Annabel Graham lives in Dunsandel and thought, 'Wouldn't it be great to have our own store?' The next thing you know it is more than 10 years on and the Dunsandel Store has become another one of those institutions that you simply must visit. **Besides providing postal and dry-cleaning services, as well as provisions for the locals, it is a café with fresh, simple and wholesome food.** Ben takes a shine to the place and decides to try the cold chocolate drink, not something you want to be having if you're on a diet.

The café is licensed and they make their own apple juice and cider from the apples off an orchard down the road. We try the cider and, not ones for drinking, notice it won't be long before we won't be able to drive. While browsing the store Matthew came across the Dunsandel Store's very own cookbook, called *A Year's Worth*. We suspect the idea for their cookbook came about over a glass or two of cider. Matthew and Ben take a shine to the fart recipe in particular, both being men who do. It is a quirky book with not only great recipes but also important bits of information. If you ever need to know how to kill a hare, this is your book. Drop in for a coffee and something to eat, get your dry-cleaning done and have a look at the occasional flea market.

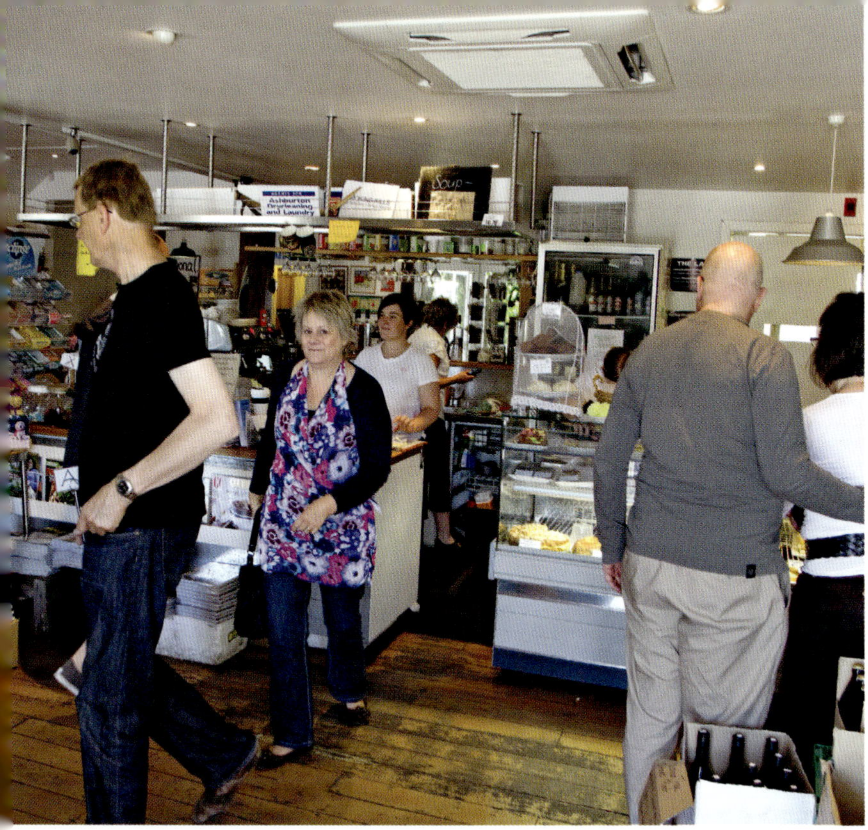
Ashburton
Drycleaning
and Laundry
Soup

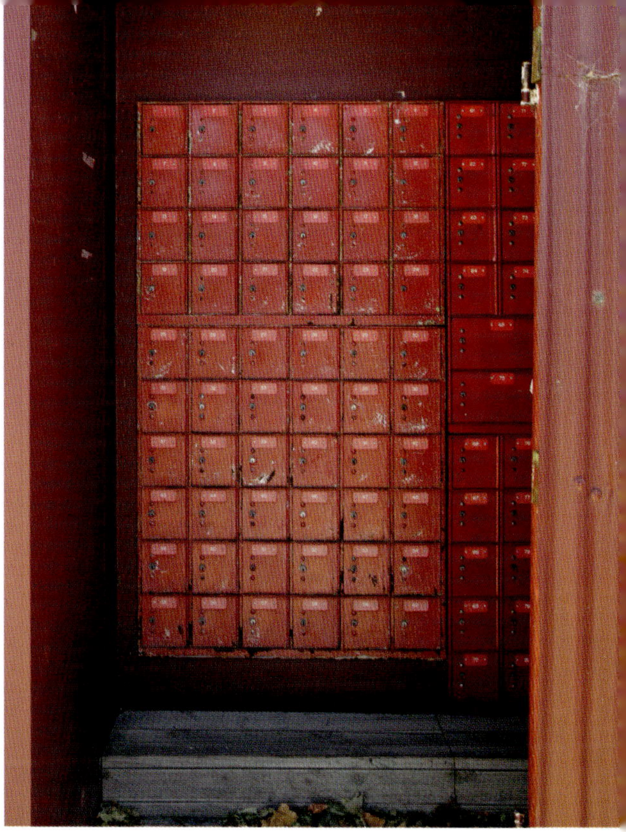

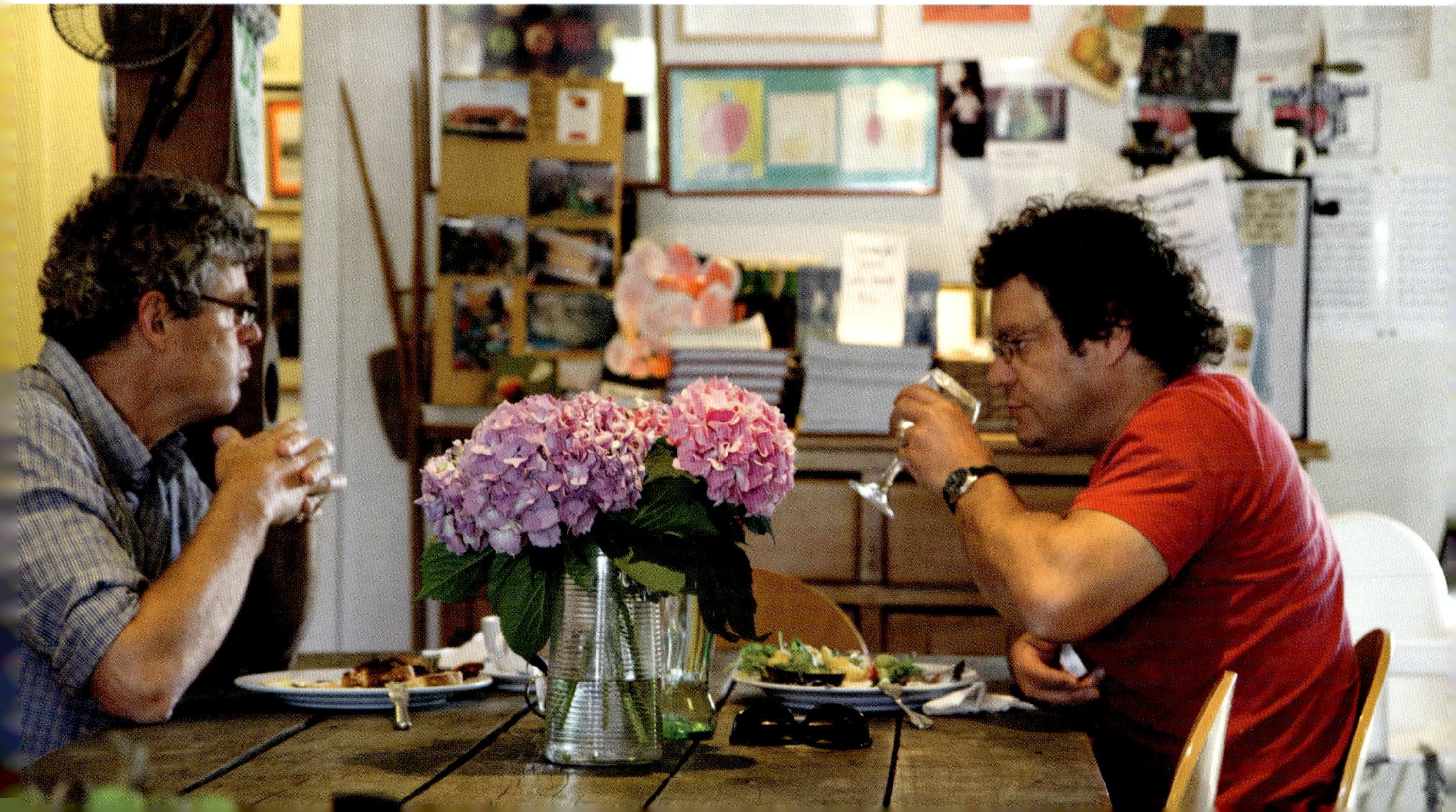

When they leave Dunsandel they have to take the back roads as the Rakaia Bridge is closed due to flooding. Floods, earthquakes — no wonder Southerners are a tough breed. Matthew and Ben love driving, and taking the back roads just makes it all the more fun. By the time they get to Methven, a popular ski town, Matthew has his doubts whether the town will have anything open. Does anyone come here outside the ski season? Well, yes they do, and Primo E Secundo is humming.

# PRIMO E SECUNDO

**38 McMillan Street**
**METHVEN**

**ALLPRESS**

When we ask the owner Marya Tengrove to sum up what her café is all about, she asks the question, 'Didn't you read the poem as you came in?'

> **The Primo E Secundo Poem**
> *Come in and take a look*
> *Have a cuppa and read a book*
> *Buy a present*
> *Tip the staff*
> *Eat some cake and have a laugh*
> *Kia Ora to one and all*

This place is a little crazy. First there was the shop that sold curios, all the items Marya had collected over the years. Then came the café in about 2004, and finally the wall between the two was knocked down to make it one fine place to visit. **Absolutely everything is for sale, and there is a lot of absolutely everything.**

Marya comes from a family of five sisters. One of them has Café Florentines in Auckland, and the two cafés couldn't be any more different. Marya's history is in catering; she catered for the Lord of the Rings crew when it was filmed there. She assures us that Hobbits are very real. Open seven days from 7 am to around 5.30 pm, Primo E Secundo is a popular destination to come and browse, have great coffee and get a little crazy.

## HELLO·HELLO!

Allpress welcomes you to a......

- Short Black $2½
- Long Black $3½
- Macciato $3
- Flat white $3½
- Latte $4
- Cappuccino $3½
- Mochaccino
- hot Chocolate /mugs
- Chai $4½

- Selection of teas- $3½
  english Breakfast, earl grey,
  green, Herbal
- Smoothies-banana, berry $5
- Iced Chocolate, Coffee, chai
- Regular T/A $4½ $5
- Large T/A $5
- Extra shot/decaf/soya/
  vanilla/caramel
  add 50cents

We leave the craziness behind, with a fantastic salmon bagel in our tummies, and head back to Christchurch. Ben needs to catch a plane and Matthew a ferry. Before the family all head off to their respective homes we decide on an afternoon tea at Sweethearts. Matthew's sister Jessica has recommended it and the kids can pick their own berries.

# SWEETHEARTS AT BERRYFIELDS

**161 Gardiners Road, Harewood**
**CHRISTCHURCH 8051**

### VIVACE

Okay, so Sweethearts isn't a traditional café, but that's what makes New Zealand special — we can sell coffee anywhere and make it work. Having a day with all of Matthew's family together doesn't happen very often and the setting couldn't have been more perfect.

Sweethearts has been operated by the Harrow family since 1991, evolving from a business dating back to the early 1900s. **You can walk around picking your own berries and when you're finished sit in the gardens under the trees — an absolutely fabulous place — enjoy a coffee and desserts to die for.**

The best way to describe Sweethearts is pretty; its surroundings, the desserts, and the girls serving.

Sitting around the table, shaded by a canopy of trees and catching up like old times, make this experience one of the more memorable of the trip. Having family and being in love with them over good coffee and desserts doesn't get any better than this.

From Christchurch, heading north to Picton, we pass the Brick Mill Café and the amazing building that used to manufacture hay bale twine, then on to the Nor'Wester Café.

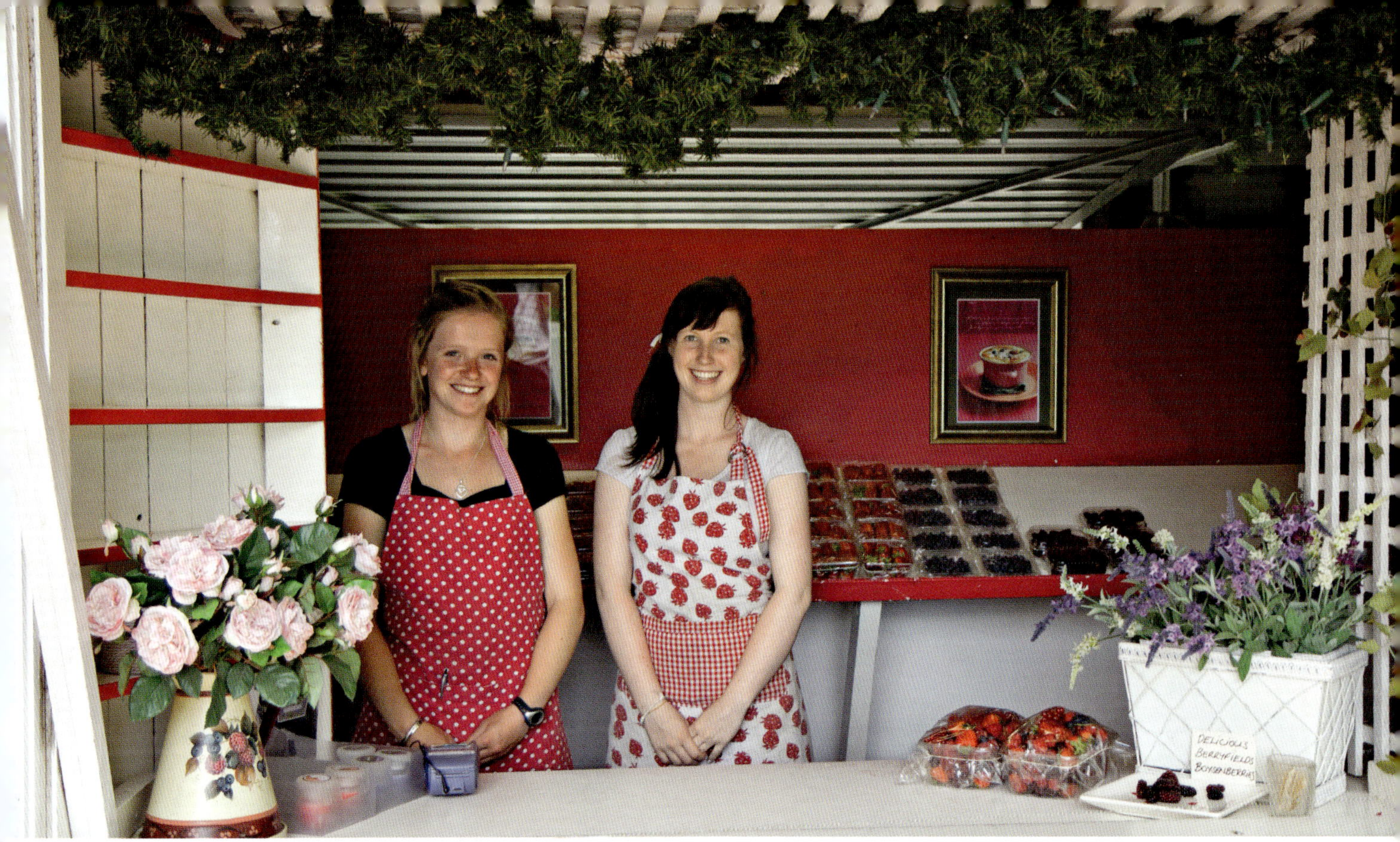
DELICIOUS
BERRYFIELDS
BOYSENBERRIES

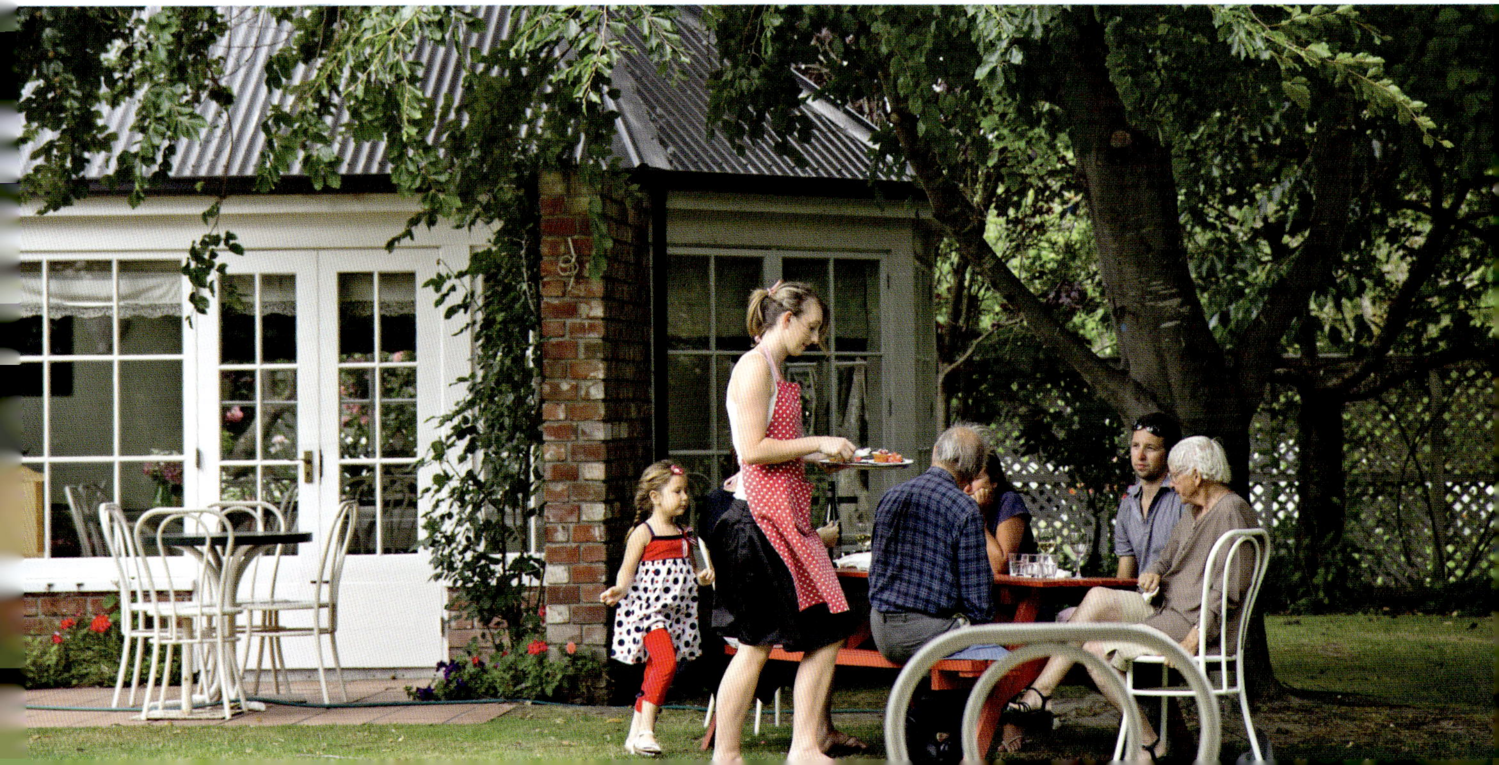

It's not long before we hit Amberley and the famous Nor'Wester Café. We walk up a brick path past palm trees and into an elegant oasis.

# NOR'WESTER CAFÉ

**95 Main North Road
AMBERLEY**

**SUPREME**

Trish Coleman is a woman of drive, passion and wisdom all wrapped up in a very likeable package. She and husband Tim own the Nor'Wester Café and we are sure Tim is a good bloke too, we just don't meet him.

Trish and Tim set up the Nor'Wester with Paul and Anne Gillman who had been based in Australia but were ready for a change. Fourteen years later Trish and Tim are going it alone. The café was two years in the planning, focusing on the potential customer base and tapping into the advice of mentors Viv and Tom Fox. Often café owners wing it and it sometimes works, but these guys did their homework and made sure the business made sense.

The first task was to hire great staff for the kitchen. In the time they have been open they have only had three head chefs; currently Sarah has been on site for nearly six of those years. The food here is ordered from a menu and not from the counter, which is confusing for some. **One of Trish's wise statements is that 'to define something is to limit it' and so although some aspects of Nor'Wester are café and others are restaurant, they blend well and the mix works.**

The food is definitely quality, served with style and is often something new to the palate — good new. Trish and Tim try to support local suppliers and will always look locally first when choosing produce. As long as supply is consistent, the local will win over outsiders.

One of the winning aspects of this café is the dedication to service and attention to the interaction between people, food and beverage. The service is fantastic and the unofficial motto is 'bugger the customer; nothing comes before the food and coffee'. This by no means makes the service bad — it is great, and led by great food and coffee.

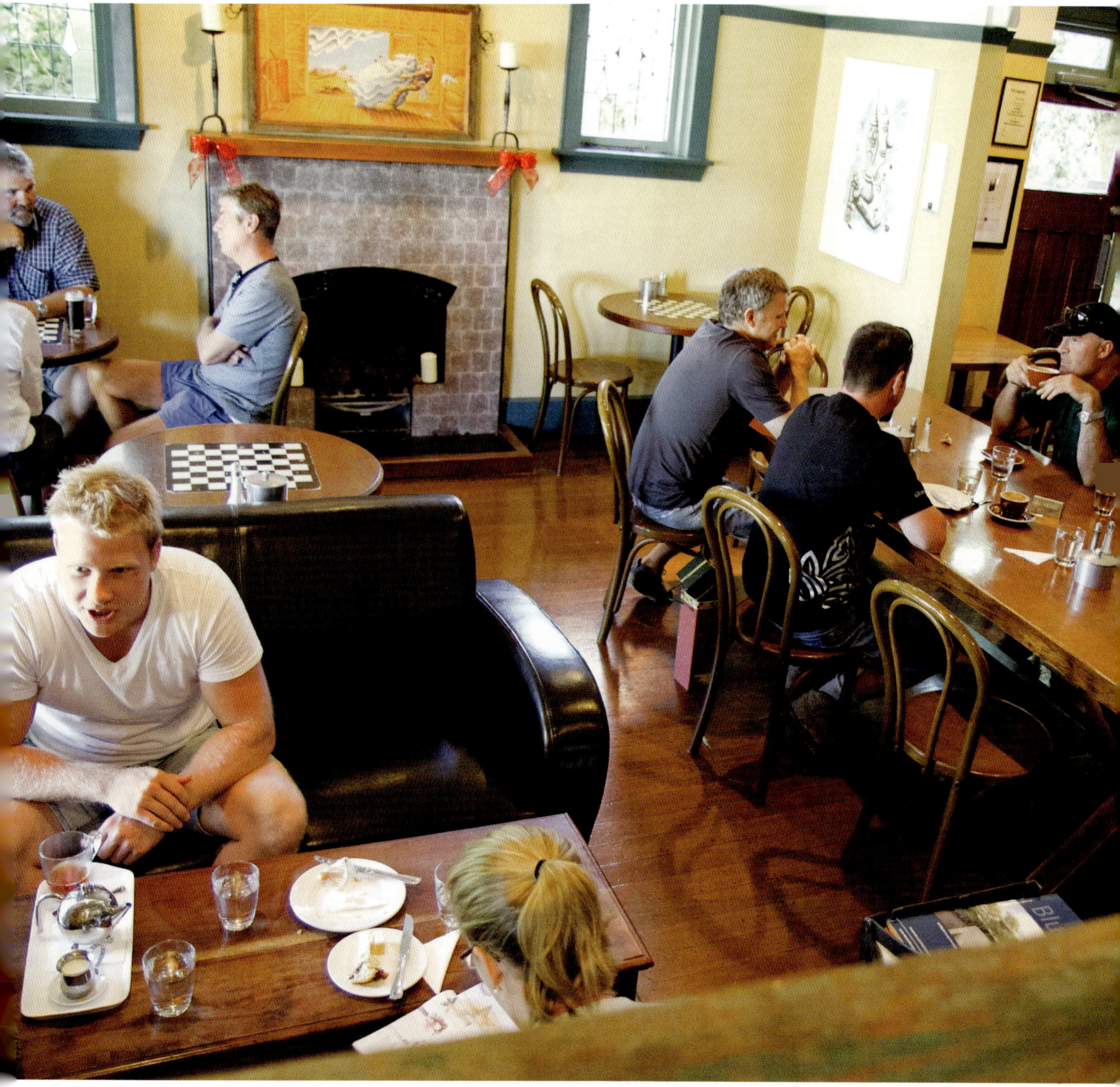

In the five hours it takes to get to Picton we pass the Cheviot Tearooms which has possibly the first espresso machine in the south. Tired and glad to be out of the car, we are back on the Interislander to meander through the sounds and back into Wellington harbour. Being the end of the day we are lucky to have Wellington greet us with a sunset. It's time to explore the city that some regard as the coffee mecca of New Zealand.

# MIDNIGHT ESPRESSO

**178 Cuba Street**
**WELLINGTON**

## HAVANA

Midnight Espresso opened in 1987. Tim and Geoff, the Havana Boys, had the place for 10 years and spawned many a café and café addict along the way before selling it to current owner Hamish McIntyre.

Wellington is an interesting experience because for a time we were under the impression that all coffee roads lead back to here. In some ways it is true. This particular branch of coffee culture in Wellington is large and entrenched. Hamish went to primary school with Tim and Geoff; also with his floor manager Nicole, whose mother does the books.

Midnight Espresso was the first of its type in Wellington. **Loud music, and a culture driven by ever-changing generations of students who sometimes evolve into establishment types but still return for their coffee, gives space for a diverse customer base. Great coffee and food is at the heart of Midnight Espresso.**

The systems in place are unusual for hospitality. The person who greets you from behind the counter will dish up your counter food, put any kitchen order through, make your coffee and take your money. In most cafés you will find specific staff holding only one or two of these roles. What strikes us about this system is the relationship with the customers it creates. The coffee maker is not removed from the customer and we think this gives the coffee extra quality. Similarly, the chef runs the food to the tables unless they are really busy. This means that the relationship exists there too.

Much of the food is vegetarian and they were using organic milk and cheese long before it became the thing to do. That's the way it is with Midnight Espresso — they do their own thing that works and is often emulated by those who have followed in their longstanding footsteps.

## MIDNIGHT ESPRESSO'S VEGAN CHOCOLATE CAKE

1 cup soya oil
1 cup soy milk
1 cup coffee syrup
½ cup 'Kara' thick coconut cream
¼ cup defrosted berries — blackberries or boysenberries are best

1 ¾ cups flour
1 ½ cups white sugar
¾ cup sifted cocoa powder
1 teaspoon baking soda
1 ½ teaspoons baking powder

½ cup berry jam

### ICING
1 cup margarine
¾ cup sifted cocoa powder
3 cups icing sugar
½ cup hot coffee

Preheat oven to 180ºC. Mix the wet and dry ingredients separately and then pour the wet mix into a 'well' in the dry mix. Mix gently by hand until a batter forms; mix as little as possible. Divide the mix between two 20 cm cake pans lined with baking paper. Bake for 20 minutes or until a skewer comes out from the cake clean. When cool join the layers of cake together with berry jam, then coat with icing.

To make the icing, beat margarine and cocoa powder together and add icing sugar, followed by coffee. The texture of the icing should be soft as the cake is delicate and firm icing may damage the cake. Enjoy.

# ROASTING

In 1656 there were complaints against a local barber who was roasting and selling a drink called coffee. It had a vile smell and the fire used for the roasting had on occasion caught the chimney alight. This is a tale from England, but it is interesting to note that Robert Harris, one of the forerunners of roasting in New Zealand, was also a barber.

Rumour has it that a man named David Strange ground his own coffee in Invercargill in the late 19th century. Then along came William Gregg who emigrated to New Zealand and set up Gregg's Coffee by the turn of the century. But coffee was not always well received — there were those who thought that it caused deranged vision and mental excitation and was not to be trusted, while others thought it was good for keeping those awake who had been poisoned by opium. Guess things were a little different in those days.

By the 1960s coffee was cool and there were the likes of Old Mill, Faggs and Stewart's coffee. Then along came Robert Harris, who began roasting coffee in Hamilton. It wasn't long before his beans were being used across the country, and the modern-day coffee shop sprang into being.

By the 1980s and 1990s boutique roasters were appearing — the likes of Millers and Allpress in Auckland, L'affare and Havana in Wellington, and C4 and Underground in Christchurch. There were no more than a dozen roasters by this time, but jump to 2010 and there were over 100. Each has a unique story and all are passionate about providing high quality beans, and as far as we can ascertain, being the best in the world.

There are the likes of Supreme, who have the enviable position of being the bean supplier to many of the top cafés in Melbourne, as reported in the Melbourne Coffee Review of 2010. In the Coromandel bush you can find Mark Tugendhaft making his local roast Coffee LaLa. We visit Mark. It takes us a while to find him — you go down a track and stop at the old shed. Mark makes his own roasters, along with multi/multi plugs hanging off the wall. For Mark this is an art, not a technology, and he has that look about him of someone who 'just knows' when the bean is ready.

At the other end of the scale of precision when roasting coffee, you can use colour coding to roast to a precise temperature. Each roaster has their own technique for roasting and although they vary in technical skill, the end result is some of the best coffee in the world.

The beans that we use in New Zealand come from across the globe — Africa, Jamaica and even New South Wales. The closest locally grown bean is around some of the islands around New Zealand. Vanuatu grows beans and, as you read earlier, C1 in Christchurch is working with Samoa to help them cultivate a commercially viable crop. It's great to hear that they have been successful and in 2011 the new C1 blend came into being, all made with beans from Samoa.

There are single origin beans, and beans that are blended, but the story that we would like to finish this little bit about roasting is the story of Havana — the coffee roasting company formed by Tim Rose and Geoff Marsland in 1989. For us this is the typical kiwi story of creating a little something different by not following the rules and reaping the benefits. When the Havana boys opened a café in Cuba St, they wanted to call it Havana Coffee Lounge, in recognition of the capital of Cuba. It ended up that they didn't but instead it became Midnight Espresso to signify its late opening hours.

They decided to roast their beans on top of the building — well at least until they almost burnt down the building. On a buying trip to Jamaica they saw Cuba just across the way and thought to themselves, 'I bet those guys have great beans.' With the American trade embargo and travel restrictions it was difficult to get into the country, but get in they did. They tried the beans and bought some of their own to check against, just to make sure they were not getting caught up in the vibe of the place. They weren't and before you knew it they had built a relationship and became the exclusive importers for Cuban beans into New Zealand. The Cubans lovingly refer to the Havana boys as just boys, and they love how New Zealand has embraced the Cuban way of life. How could we have not — salsa, sex and style — what's not to like?

> **In the Coromandel bush you can find Mark Tugendhaft making his local roast Coffee LaLa . . . For Mark this is an art, not a technology, and he has that look about him of someone who 'just knows' when the bean is ready.**

A little walk down Cuba Mall and down a side lane, you will come across a café emanating Italian style that Niki fell in love with. It's a little unusual for New Zealand, a stylish boutique café full of European men with moustaches and deep voices.

# DUKE CARVELL'S SWAN LANE EMPORIUM

**6 Swan Lane
WELLINGTON**

### L'AFFARE

Leonardo and Lorenzo Bresolin stem from a family that has long been established in hospitality in Wellington. Their dad Remiro arrived in New Zealand from Italy and opened the first pizza place in town in 1972, before going on to open the famous Il Casino restaurant, and the boys grew up in the business.

Sadly their dad has passed away and yet we imagine he would be very proud of where the boys, now men, have followed in his footsteps. One of their bases is Duke Carvell's Swan Lane Emporium and it has a flavour unlike any we have seen around the country.

**There is a rich quality to the eatery with books, paintings and other bits that draw you into a European frame of mind.**
During the day they 'play to the crowd', providing extensions of what you might expect regarding food, teamed with dining-related drinks. The French, Italian and Spanish direction is built upon in the evening with deconstructed dinners. You are likely to share a table full of a number of dishes, reminiscent of a large family dinner, rather than a plate that's yours exclusively.

Duke Carvell was a man who by all accounts lived life to the full — enjoying the fine things in life. It appears that the Bresolin men have named their establishment in honour of that. The coffee here is excellent and the calibre of handsome men who serve makes Niki blush. The photo on the door near the back of the building is of Leonardo and Lorenzo's father at the age of 22, just before he left Italy for New Zealand — he also seems to have the look that turns the ladies' heads. Long may the tradition of hospitality excellence spiced with a bit of European flair continue . . .

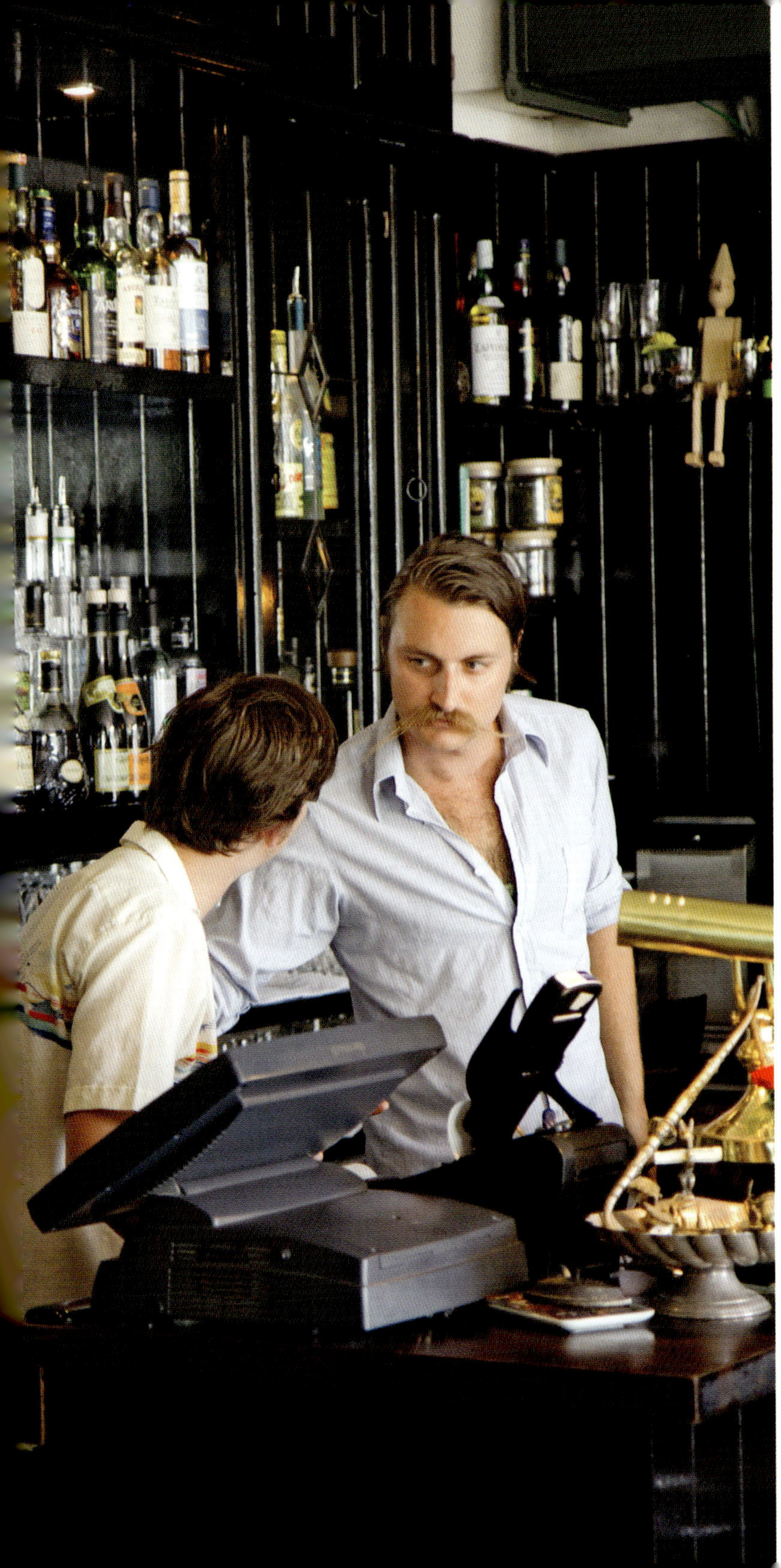

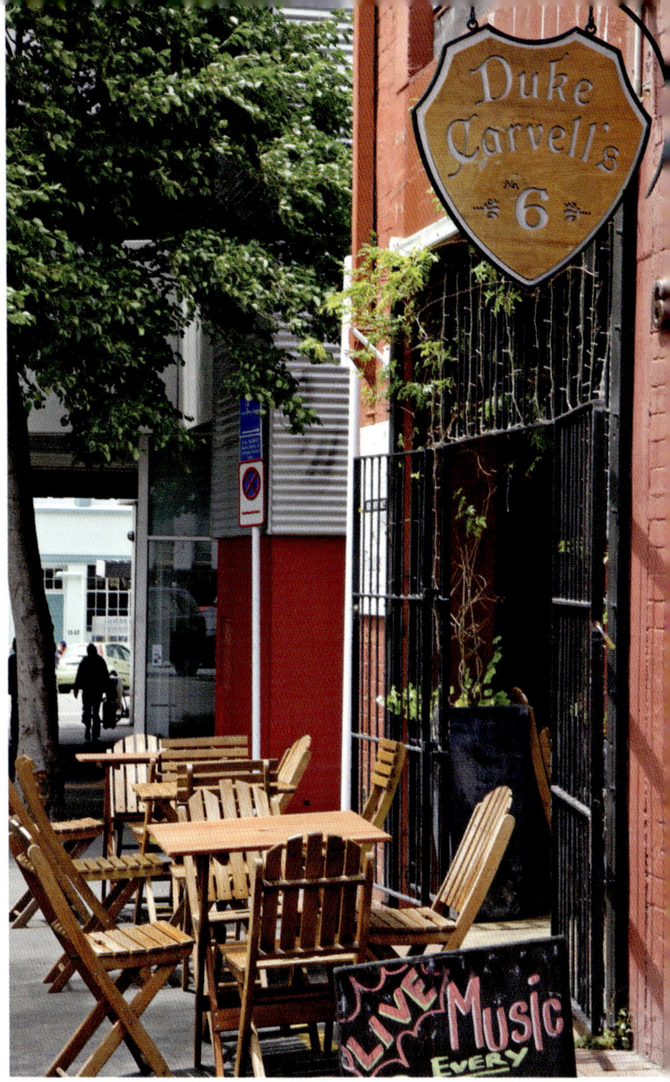
Duke Carvell's
6
LIVE Music
EVERY

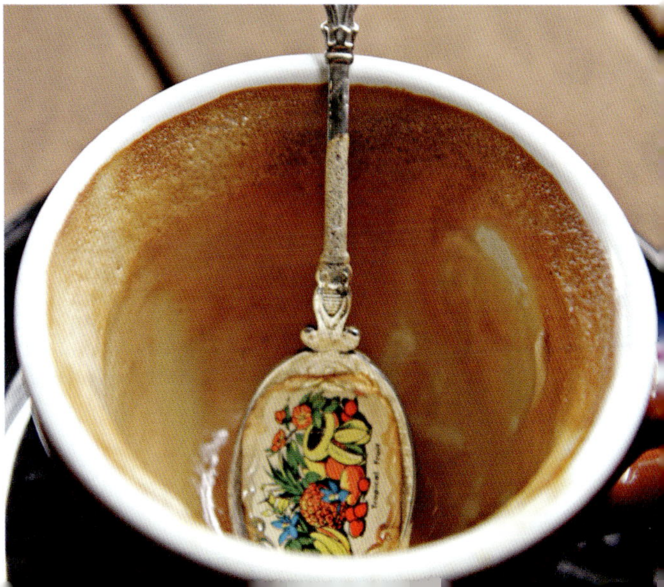

Our next day we are back with kids and decide to head out of the city and pay a visit to one of the local beaches. We have heard about a surf club café, and on the way is the Weta Cave in Miramar, a mini museum that shows behind-the-scenes footage of the Weta studios, home to Peter Jackson and the Lord of the Rings movies.

# MARANUI CAFÉ

**The Parade, Lyall Bay**
**WELLINGTON**

### HAVANA

Herein lies another Wellington scene connection. Maranui Café is owned by Matt Wilson, Katie Richardson and Bronwyn Kelly. Matt started in the hospitality world at the ripe old age of 17 when he opened Kiaora Coffee Lounge in Vivian Street. At the same time he helped supply pinball machines around the city. As a result he spent much time at Midnight Espresso playing on the machine, developing a love of coffee and a relationship with Tim and Geoff.

Next stop: Deluxe Café, purchased from the Havana dynasty when he's still only 18. One year later Katie joins the business and they are heading for 20 years at the Deluxe Café. In 2004 the Maranui Surf Life Saving Club wanted to encourage a larger membership and hit upon the idea of a café. Matt and Katie loved the idea and were in; Bronwyn joined the partnership and the business began.

In the early days you had to pay to be a member of the surf club and sign in to go to the café. Membership then became free, and numbers swelled to 30,000 — the largest club membership in New Zealand.

All was going swimmingly until disaster struck in August 2009 when the building was severely damaged in a nasty fire. The building was owned by the council and they were not prepared to rebuild, so the campaign began with huge publicity and public meetings. Eventually the surf club took ownership of the building and the council helped rebuild. **We sit watching the interisland ferry pass by in the distance, drinking our coffee and enjoying the cool atmosphere.** The cabinet looks great; Katie is an amazing cook with a specialty in salads.

1911
EXIT

PALM READER
TRY ME I TALK!
THE ZOLTAR PALM READER

Jantzen
Be attractive
while you're active

On our last day we take a drive well out of the city and up to Waikanae on the Kapiti Coast, and another beach. We've driven through Waikanae many times before on the way to Wellington but didn't even know there was a beach, but here it is with a great café too.

# THE FRONT ROOM

**42 Tutere Street**
**WAIKANAE BEACH**

**SUPREME**

From a foodie perspective this place is a little bit of heaven in a surprising location. As we walk through the converted building into the outdoor seating area we can tell we are on to a good thing. The girls (Ruby made a friend) settle in beanbags while we commandeer a large table, spreading out with computers and paper to do some work using the free wireless internet.

**The Front Room is humming with customers arriving in a steady stream; the coffee machine located in a hut/bar set up in the back is bubbling away and the buzz becomes clear when we eat the food. It's divine.** The kids are satisfied by their very own menu that provides all the things that kids like at a café, and then they go to the beach. Sandcastles and wet clothes are calling.

Owners Craig McBrearty and Hilary Bowen returned from working in London and saw potential in this café for sale. One of the reasons for placing themselves off the beaten track was to allow time to learn how to run the business out of the limelight, with space for the odd mistake (inevitable despite Craig's 20 years in the trade). Another was to get a feel for what New Zealand had become in their absence.

Initially the plan was to learn here and then move into a big city, but that has not happened. Nearly a decade on the café is doing well and the plan is to stay.

The customer base is from far afield in the summer months with the locals more of a feature in winter. The unusual set-up of coffee making out the back has a clever purpose. During summer a number of beachgoers want takeaway coffee and the café becomes congested. In order to accommodate everyone happily, you can now go around the side for your takeaway and in through the front should you need more.

We finish our time here and head down to the beach to watch Ruby and Emma fully clad swim in the sea. A good memory.

## THE FRONT ROOM'S
## HALOUMI SALAD

3 medium beetroot
3 tablespoons red wine vinegar
3 tablespoons olive oil
2 red onions, sliced
2 cloves garlic, chopped
½ teaspoon sumac
3 cups bulgar wheat
1 ¾ cups chicken or vegetable stock
½ cup quinoa
1 cup roasted almonds, skin on, roughly chopped
1 cup chopped fresh herbs (flat parsley, mint, dill, chives, sage)
juice of 2 lemons
salt and pepper to taste
250 g haloumi

Preheat oven to 180°C. Wrap beetroot in foil and bake in oven for 30 minutes or until cooked. Chop into wedges, cover with red wine vinegar and leave to cool.

Heat oil in pan, sauté red onions, garlic and sumac. Add bulgar wheat and stir to combine. Add stock, one ladle at a time, stirring continuously, until wheat is firm to the bite but not hard. Once cooked, spoon on to a flat tray and leave to cool.

Cook quinoa as per instructions on packet and allow to cool. Combine bulgar wheat, quinoa, almonds and fresh herbs with lemon juice, seasoning and extra virgin olive oil if liked.

Serve the bulgar wheat and quinoa, place four wedges of beetroot on top of the wheat mixture and add two slices of seared haloumi per portion.

*Finally, after almost a week of staying in a tenth-floor apartment, it is time to head back into the countryside and explore the towns. We leave the city lights and Wellington wind and head towards Greytown. It's not long before we get there, where we find a freshly roasted, delightful espresso, a beautiful tearoom selling high teas and a plethora of boutique stores. The Main Street Deli has been recommended, and the sign says it won an award so in we go.*

# MAIN STREET DELI & CAFÉ

**88 Main Street**
**GREYTOWN**

### VITTORIA

**Busy, busy, busy . . . and some more busy.** Through the door of Main Street Deli & Café we find an abundance of people. They just keep coming. We seat ourselves near the front counter in order to check out the food and catch the eye of the owner should there be a break. There isn't one. We eat and drink fine food and coffee, but still there's no space to intake breath and ask for some time. Eventually Niki gives up waiting and heads into the deli section hoping for more luck. That comes in the form of Glenys Almao, one of the partners in the business; the other is Gerald Brown but on this day he is out of town.

Glenys is cooking in the deli, serving customers and talking to Niki all at the same time — a multi-tasker extraordinaire. Both Glenys and Gerald come from Wellington's hospitality world. Glenys has lived in Greytown since the late 1990s and realised there was a space in the market for a good deli. Food is the focus, with much made on site and tempting goodies arriving from around New Zealand and the world at regular intervals.

Two-thirds of business done here is over the summer months, leaving the winter free to stock up on making preserves and travelling to find new and exciting products to stock the deli with. Travelling in this way has inspired Glenys's other passion, Bali. She has become involved in importing palm sugar, fragrant peppers and other Balinese delights.

Kereru are plentiful in this beautiful area and rivers and a temperate climate add to the mix. If you get here, make your way to the Deli and try one of their famous pies, on site or takeaway. That's what we did, took a pie and added our salad for the main and then some great yoghurt and Hawke's Bay fruit for dessert . . . scrumptious.

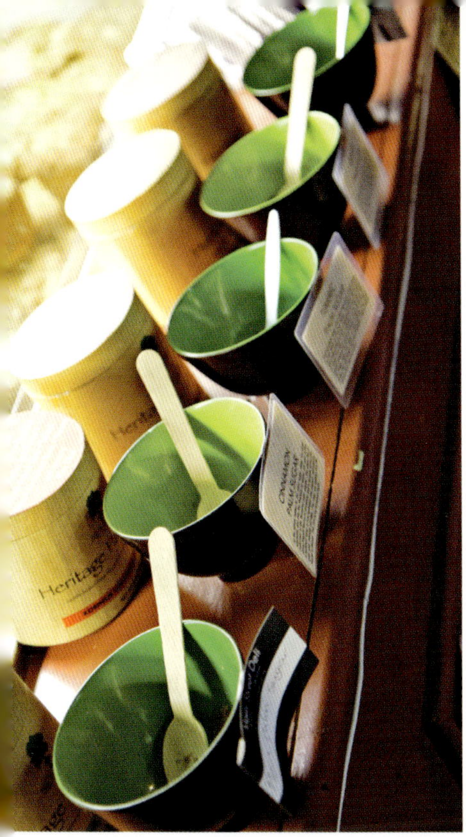
Heritage

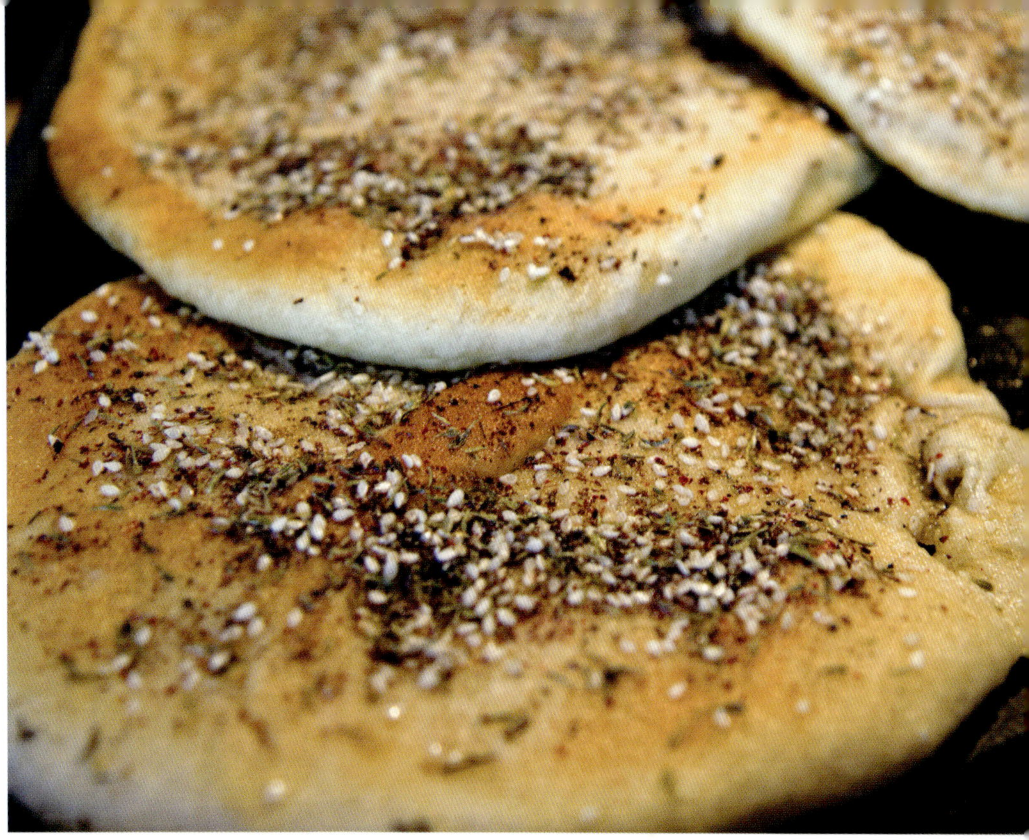

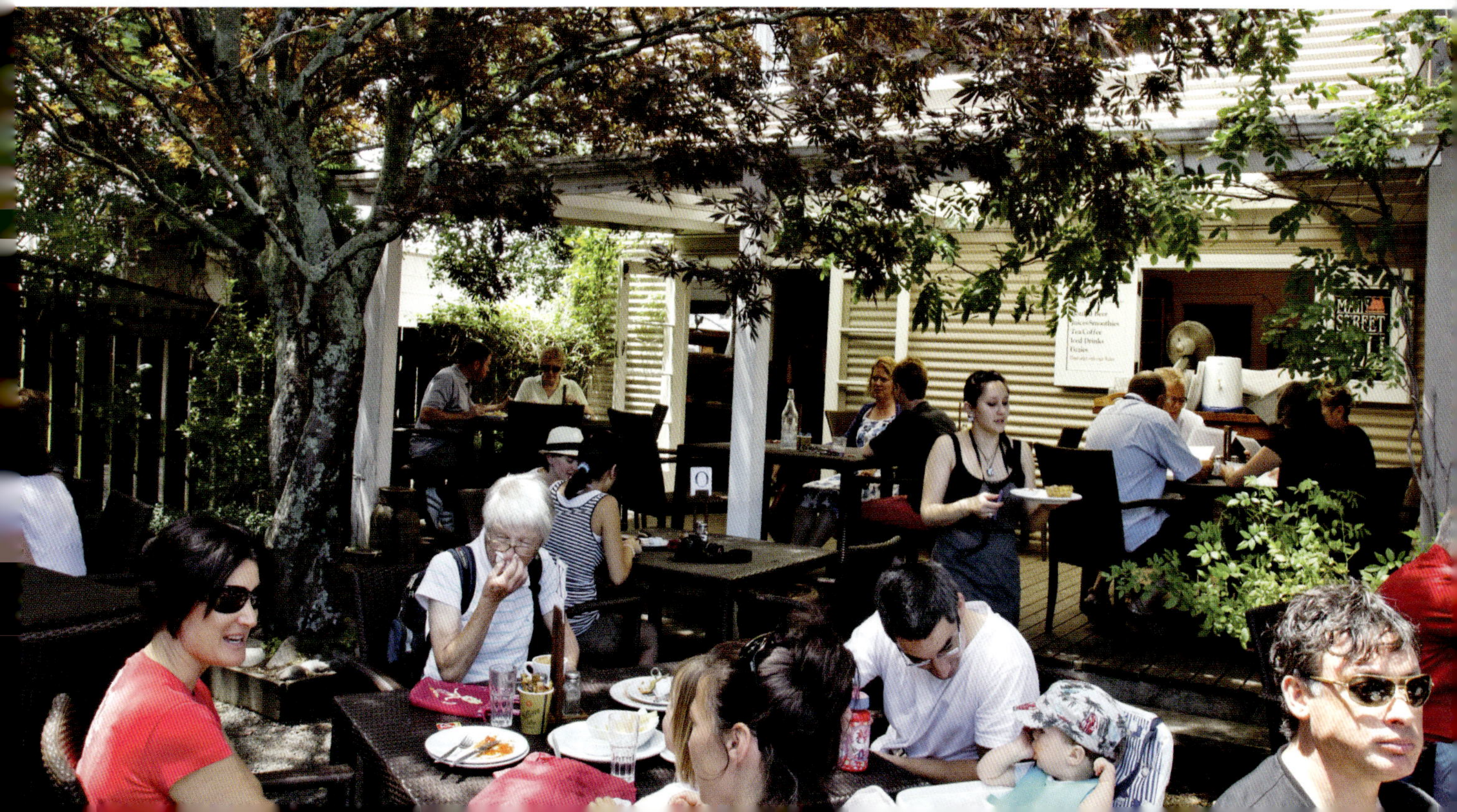

Leaving Greytown behind, we head north to Hawke's Bay. We figure there won't be that many cafés, only one or two good ones, but again we end up being completely wrong. Just outside Hastings we come across a café that has been recommended.

# THE PAPER MULBERRY CAFÉ & ART GALLERY

**State Highway 2, Pukehou**
**20 MINUTES SOUTH OF HASTINGS**

## HAVANA

Named after the aute tree that arrived with Maori in the migratory canoes, The Paper Mulberry Café is a blend of culture — Maori and Pakeha in many ways. Located directly across the road from the now shell-like Te Aute College, this café is one centre of a longstanding community. Lynne and Dave Robertson are at the heart of that centre and their commitment to the community is huge.

Dave was a police officer for 30 years and Lynne most recently taught swimming in town. When Dave decided he had had enough, he and Lynne went on a bike tour around the South Island hanging out in cafés and discussing what the next part of their lives would be.

On returning home they bought the local hall that was owned by the church. The building was originally set up as a Sunday school in 1859 by Lydia Williams; in 1952 it became the community hall, housing craft fairs, playgroups and the local theatrical group.

**Lynne has a way with food and the coffee is just as good. The thing that is most interesting about The Paper Mulberry, though, is not the food and coffee but the spirit of the people involved.** The café provides employment for four people from the small area, as well as part-time work for some of the youth. Dave and Lynne figure that if they can give the local kids some skills to transfer to the city when they go to university, it's a good start.

There's also the bookshop out the back, where second-hand books are donated. All the proceeds, on average $3000 a year, go to helping local adults return to study. Lynne makes a mean roast and the café has monthly dinners for those from the community who are not involved in the local school.

Without the school links, some people might become isolated; at these dinners they can connect with others in the community — and they do in big numbers. An open microphone night on the last Friday of every month draws in crowds of up to 70 people. And if that wasn't enough, the café also sells craft and art on behalf of local artists. The community must have known that Lynne and Dave were going to be an asset because they all pitched in to renovate the building prior to opening. The outside of the building was completely painted with two coats in just two days.

Leaving the Mulberry it takes another half an hour to get to Havelock North, only to find an abundance of good cafés. There is a popular local roaster called Hawthorne with a little espresso bar for a great coffee. Down the road, and around the corner, is Adam and Eva's Café and Food Store, another great place, and we buy some deli items for later. From Havelock North to Hastings is only five minutes. We spot the grand Opera House, where we can imagine high society opera nights, all glam and glee. The sense of sophistication is unexpected, and the café is another treasure we have found.

# OPERA KITCHEN

312 Eastbourne Street
HASTINGS

### ALLPRESS

People who have been in cafés for a long time and have high standards regarding service and food know a kindred spirit when they see one, and this is what Niki finds in Jennifer Le Comte, owner and in-house magic maker at Opera Kitchen.

Jennifer is well connected to Auckland's café scene: she shared ownership of successful deli Crucial Traders in Kingsland when it was great, and can name many of the original players as her acquaintances. On returning to Hawke's Bay after a stint in Australia, Jennifer discovered that the area had some nice restaurants but no great cafés. A restaurant chef by trade, she wanted to create a more relaxed atmosphere with quality food.

After two and a half years looking for the perfect location, a space adjacent to the Opera House became available and was so good it was impossible to turn it down. It's now Opera Kitchen. All the great aspects of the surrounding area — its produce, wine, weather, arts and design — are reduced to their essence and encompassed in the café and its food.

The food here is strictly seasonal, for however long the produce is naturally available for — fortnightly if that's what it is. Jennifer visits the market and creates the menu around the fresh produce available, then brings it back to her kitchen and invites the customer in to join her. **To be a café or restaurant is not the desire, it is to be the home kitchen you can relax in and enjoy the fabulous food.** The customers seem to like the concept, with mothers' groups and corporate meetings taking place in the same space, sometimes with the same people in attendance.

Opera Kitchen is open for Opera House events but other than that the hours tend to be daytime and busy. Jennifer is her own classic customer who wants new, healthy and light food, and if she is going to eat it . . . the food must be good. We agree and this was one of only two cafés we had to go back to for a second taste, the other being Food at Wharepuke. Not because we didn't have all we needed for the book, but because we couldn't resist.

Leaving Hastings we head towards the sea and the Art Deco town of Napier. Driving in and seeing the seaside attractions, the beach and unique houses is what make Napier a little different. It's a bustling seaside town with Art Deco style buildings, not commonly seen in New Zealand, and again some great cafés.

# GROOVE KITCHEN ESPRESSO

**112 Tennyson Street,
NAPIER**

### ATOMIC AND VELOCE

Two things stand out when we think about Groove Kitchen Espresso — one is the knowledge around coffee making that sits within Ben Simcox, the other is his personality and beautiful eyes.

Ben is into both coffee and music in a big way. He has travelled the world as a barista trainer and is focused on every small detail about how to create the perfect espresso. And not only the textbook-perfect espresso — Ben is likely to know how to mess with the classic to give you exactly what you'd like.

Born and raised in Hawke's Bay, it seems that when it was time to stop moving, the call of home was heard. When Ben first returned he spent some time roasting with Bay Espresso coffee. When his current premises became available, he decided to combine a number of ideas and passions in one space. Coffee consultancy and training take place alongside the café which has Ben and his award-winning coffee-making ability at the heart. The food is also a focus and has won awards. Ben ideally has at least two to three things on the menu or in the ever-changing cabinet that customers have difficulty deciding between.

Music is a feature, with regular gigs taking place. Technology features too with the coffee espressing often being videoed and relayed to the screen or wall. Ruby was most impressed when she could access the internet and it appeared on the wall in front of her.

**Innovation is what takes place in Groove Kitchen Espresso — deconstructed tea, technology and coffee combined, coffee poured at the table, food that pops and an introduction to new artists all make up what is excellence in the bay.**

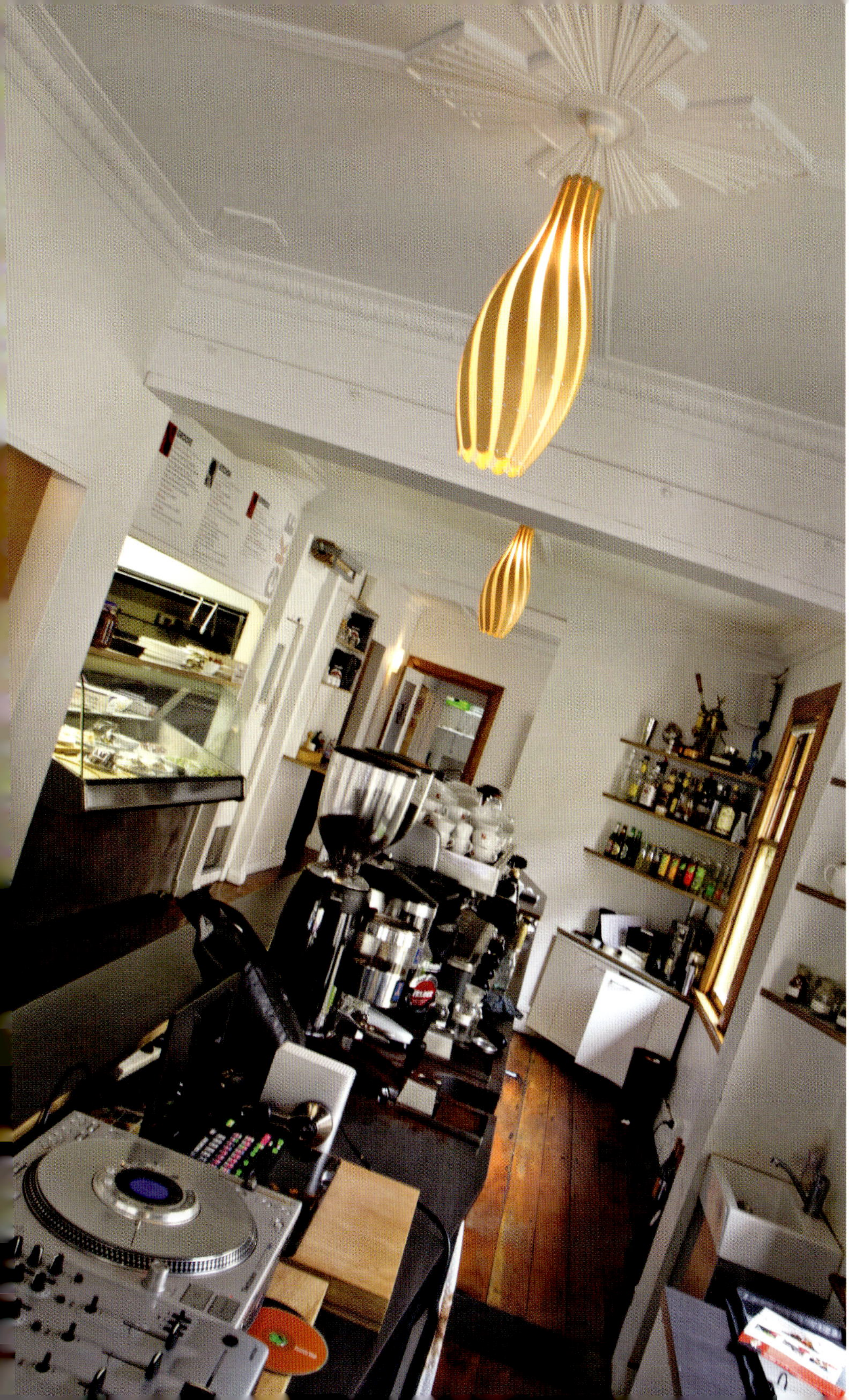

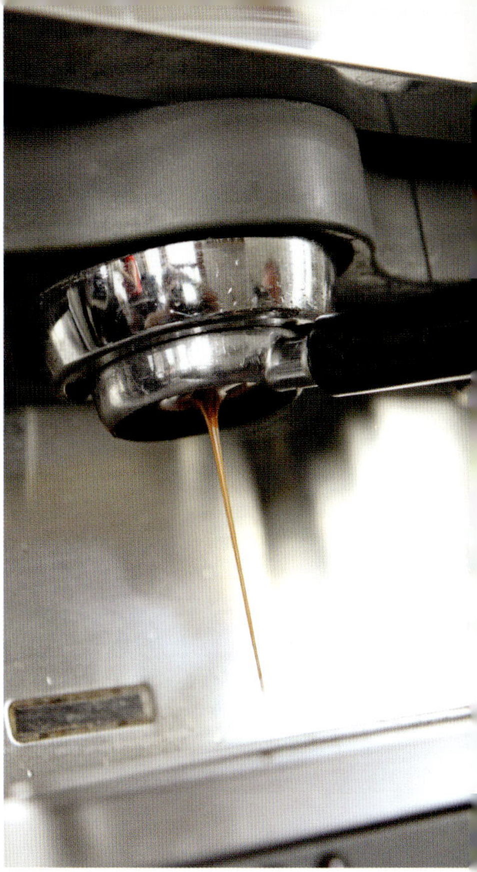

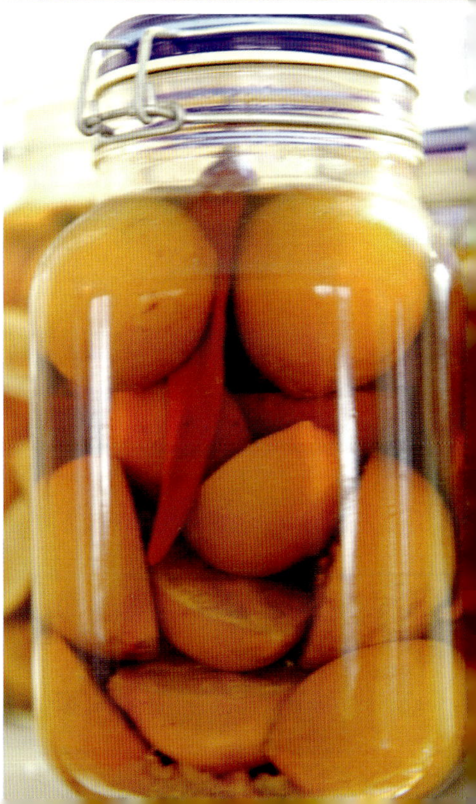

From the seaside Art Deco of Napier we stay on the coast and head north to where three rivers converge, the city of Gisborne. Whatever direction you approach it from, you travel along winding roads and the scenery is very different to Napier, yet has a sort of beachy feel with palm trees in the main street. After settling in at our accommodation, we head out to a café called Zest, which has been recommended on a number of occasions.

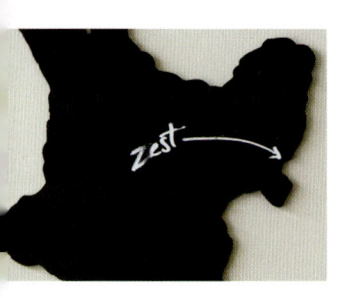

## ZEST CAFÉ

**22 Peel Street
GISBORNE**

### BAY ESPRESSO

When we walk in the door we wonder if we might be disappointed — the fit-out doesn't have the character café look; there's nothing wrong with it, it's just that nothing really catches our eye. So we order and then sit, thinking the food and coffee will be average . . . wrong with a capital W. The food is fantastic and the coffee holds its own too.

We ask to speak to an owner or manager and after some phone tag Amy Smith, who is now Amy Spense, makes her way in to meet us. On a normal day either Amy or her business partner Simon Mackintosh will be on site, but we discover this is no normal day. Amy fits us in between two wedding-oriented appointments, one of which is the first dress fitting, five days out from her wedding. She's cutting it fine.

Simon, who is not the groom in the above scenario, tends to be front of house and coffee maker, while Amy is more involved in the kitchen. They are old friends who were separately travelling the world, and discussed the idea of a café when they met up in Australia. On returning home Amy talked Simon into doing it.

**Good food and service delivered consistently are what makes this place work.** There is now a huge catering side to the business with a 650 sit-down dinner one of the largest to date. Often the catering events take place on a Saturday, and with Zest being never-endingly busy they close on Sundays so that everyone gets at least one day off per week.

## ZEST CAFÉ'S **MINT, LEMON & LIME REFRESHER**

¼ cup apple juice
juice of 1 lime
juice of 1 lemon
1 sprig mint
1 tablespoon vanilla ice cream
1 heaped teaspoon honey
½ cup ice

Blend all ingredients together and serve in a tall glass.

We leave Gisborne and decide not to drive up around the coast, as we don't have any recommendations. Our next destination is Tauranga. On the way we have one café to explore in Whakatane. Well, that's what we think. Deciding to stop at Opotiki for fish and chips changes our plans, as we find a café that will end up in the book. Matthew notices people sitting upstairs in a building — he has an eye for finding the cafés — and up the stairs we go.

# ROSTCARD'S 1914 CAFÉ

**18 King Street**
**OPOTIKI**

### EMPORIO

Pretty, pretty, pretty . . . yes it is, but even the group of local working men at their favourite table in the corner look right at home. Nora Moore-Kelly owns the café and works there at the weekend and early mornings before leaving the staff to it as she heads to her day job at Whakatohea Maori Trust board. Nora doesn't think she works particularly hard; she says the variety makes it feel like cruising.

The space is in a building named Rostgards after Danish settlers. When Nora opened the café her business cards were mistakenly printed with a c instead of a g, and she decided to leave it. So Rostcard's it is. Prior to the café there were three apartments in the space and it took three months to renovate it to its present form.

Niki reckons that toilets are a very important part of a café. If the loo is grubby or ugly she wonders what is going on behind closed doors in the kitchen. Rostcard's wins the prize for the most fabulous ladies' room we come across. There are armchairs and ornate mirrors in the powder room and it smells great. The boys' one is fine too, but Matthew doesn't think it's a scratch on the ladies'.

**With a pretty design, great bathrooms and reasonably priced cool jewellery on sale, as well as great coffee and treat-y food, Rostcard's has a feminine vibe that is also welcoming to men. We love it.**

We leave Opotiki with another feeling of having found somewhere special we weren't expecting.

1914
ROSTGARD'S
UPSTAIRS
café
Art &
Collectables
Licensed
Café

We're a little disheartened in Whakatane where a recommended café is under new ownership with a sense that they're still feeling their way. We need another good café to pick us up. And here serendipity plays its card again, as we find the Whitehouse. From the outside Matthew has his reservations, but it isn't long before we are raving about the quintessential Maori café . . .

# THE WHITEHOUSE CAFÉ

**8b Thornton Road
WHAKATANE**

**VIVACE**

A spirit of manaakitanga — loosely translated as hospitality or kindness — is one way to describe what you will find at The Whitehouse Café. **The house and family within have been in this area for generations; to work here you have to be family — and you are treated as family as soon as you walk through the door.**

Jan Hohapata-Oke and her practical, inclusive manner are at the core of this café and family. It is refreshing and interesting to hear that the cure for many ills is to put on the running shoes and get moving. This matches the upbeat feeling which hits as you walk through the door, with genuine greetings coming from the staff — all of whom are related.

The whare was in Jan's husband John's whanau for years, originally as the family home, then temporary rugby club rooms before becoming the hidden treasure it is today. The objective is to keep it in the family and provide work for the tamariki and mokopuna coming through.

There is a large outside area, both covered and uncovered, and when we visit a stage is being built to expand the opportunity for bands to play. All the family are very much into their home-grown music, and knowing this makes sense of the cool music played on location. Loving and including are the values that drive the business. At a table next to ours are a group of young German men on a surfing trip. They have stayed the night in return for doing some work around the place. They plan on being here for a few days as part of the family. Jan believes in bartering as a way for all to win, and we swap one of our first books for a lovely lunch.

Jan's customers connect very much with the Maori principles that guide the café. We feel right at home too, and look forward to returning.

Smoothies + Spirulina $6
Berry, Banana, Combo, Dairy Free
~SPECIALS~
*Panfried fresh fish served on couscous
*Bacon + Mushroom Fettucine $16
Amstel Light, Woodstock, Corona
*WHITE WINE Sauvignon Blanc, Chardonna
Pinot Gris, Riesling $7glass, Jacobs Creek
*RED WINE Merlot, Pinot Noir, Shiraz, Cabernet
*LOCAL BREW-

Tauranga is a small city, and we wonder what the café scene is like. The local radio jumps on board, and during their morning show chat about what makes a good café and ask the locals to text in their recommendations. Armed with a short list we head off to First Ave to find Grindz.

# GRINDZ CAFÉ

**50 First Avenue
TAURANGA**

**FUSION**

When we walk in we instantly enjoy the vibe; there's wood everywhere and spacious areas to sit and watch the large numbers of people who are coming through the door. As we walk up the stairs we discover one of the obvious draw cards for those with small children. There is a whole room dedicated to kids, with a half door to keep them safe and contained. **It is possible to watch your children and have adult time in one moment, a real find for the exhausted parent.**

The other thing that strikes us is the proliferation of blonde, slim, beautiful young women behind the counter. It turns out they are the daughters of the couple who own the café — Lesley and Steve Graham. Many of the cafés we visit in this trip work because family is involved. In this case it is impossible for the girls to ring in sick as they are in the same house as the boss. Lesley's mum is in charge of the shopping and as she is a serious bargain hunter it is estimated she has saved the business thousands.

This spot was originally the roastery for Fusion Coffee and café. The Grahams bought the place and the roastery moved on to leave a large space that has been filled with hearty food, great coffee, wireless internet, happy customers and one busy family.

The next morning we spend the day swimming, visit Mount Maunganui and enjoy a stroll along the boardwalk. Then it's time for Rotorua, one of the places Matthew liked to visit as a kid. He still does, and both he and Ethan have friends in the town.

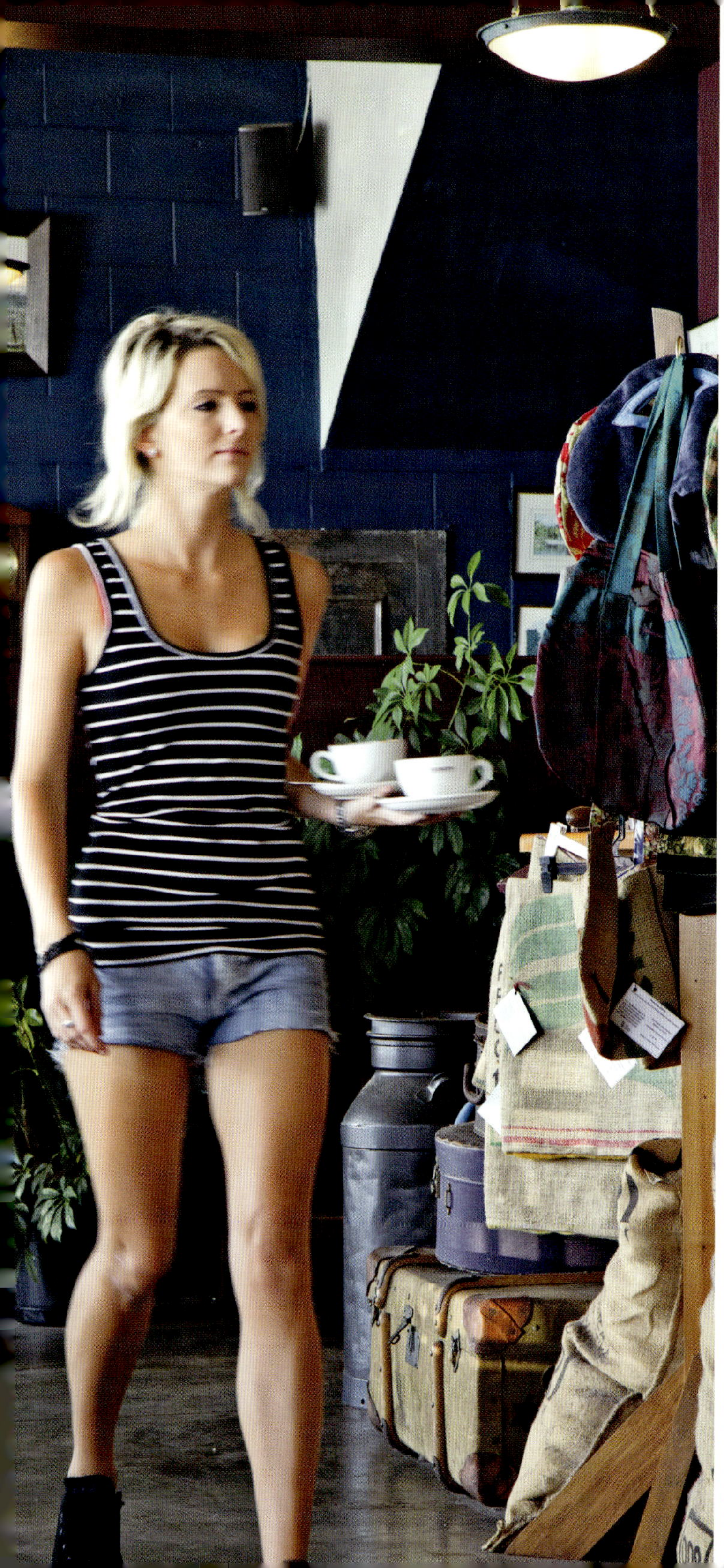
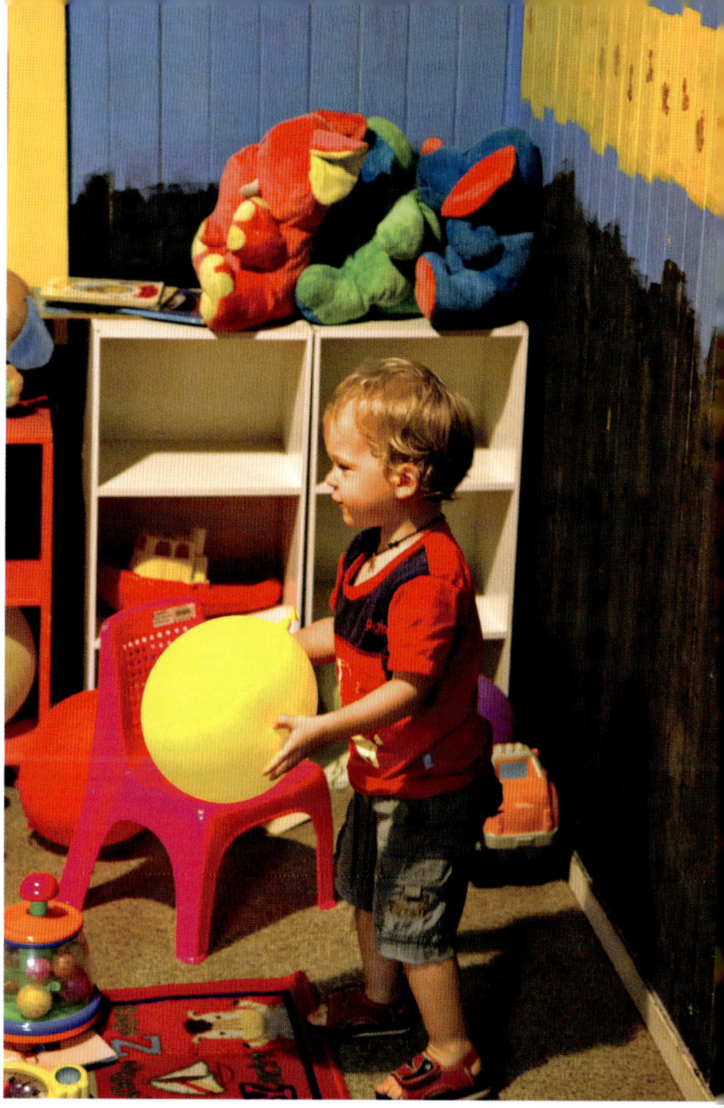
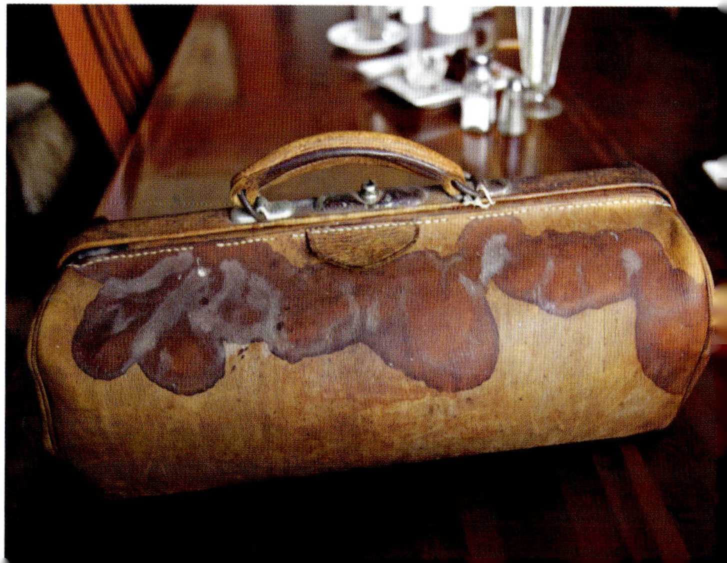

We stay at the Malfroy Motor Lodge, a divine place hidden behind motel mile. Mairi and Ron have done a fine job with this place. Ruby explores the secret gardens behind the units, and Matthew enjoys the thermal and swimming pool. Before looking around the city, we visit Okere Falls.

# OKERE FALLS STORE

**759 State Highway 33, RD 4 Okere Falls**
**ROTORUA**

## ROCKET

Niki has heard of this place and is intrigued to find out more. She has created an image in her head of what it will be like and can't wait to have her vision realised. And Okere Falls Store is exactly what Niki imagines — with a few welcome additions.

Sarah Uhl is the woman behind the store. She was the original owner of the ever popular Fat Dog in town, although she sold it many years ago. She has also opened up a new café in the town library, and that is about as close as she gets to connecting with her unused history degree.

Okere Falls Store has been a personal and community-focused project from the beginning. Sarah and her family live just down the road from the store, built by locals, but empty when she bought it in 2003. The community itself had no centre and was becoming fragmented. When Sarah made plans, the community got totally behind her and she restored the building to 1940s style and opened up what is now the town hub.

One of the things that Sarah loves most is that people from all walks of life frequent and connect in her place. There is much money tied up in the holiday homes in the area and there are also some people living a very simple, financially tight life. The two can be found chatting away over coffee at the store with social barriers dissolved.

**The store provides everyday staple requirements to go, a full menu café, a licensed venue for gigs and an annual beer festival.** Sarah and family are involved in the outdoors as a daily part of life, kayaking, pedalling and generally making use of what lies at their doorstep. Sarah and the Okere Falls Store are yet another reminder of the power we have as individuals to enhance others' lives, as well as our own, by taking part and living our dreams.

Coffee & Drinks
ESPRESSO
SM HOT CHOC
MACHIATTO
FLAT WHITE
CAPPUCCINO
MOCHACCINO
LG HOT CHOC
Chai Latte
Iced Coffee
Iced Choc
BRATWURST
SAUSAGE

Taupo, pronounced toe and paw, is about an hour's drive from Rotorua, so that's where we head the following day. It is only by chance that we hear about a café off the beaten track. We stop at Acacia Bay for a swim in the lake and Matthew has an epiphany. 'My God, we have been travelling the country for over two months, exploring the beautiful land and meeting amazing people in amazing cafés. Wow, what a fantastic journey, I don't want it to stop.' And as we stop in our next café, the wow factor just gets better.

# L'ARTE CAFÉ GALLERY

### 255 Marapa Road, Acacia Bay
### TAUPO

#### SUPREME

Judi Brennan is an award-winning artist, specialising in mosaic and ceramic works. For many years she has worked from her property close to Acacia Bay. Around 2005 Jo Brennan (Judi's daughter) and her partner Andrew Blewett joined Judi on the property, opening what is surely becoming one of the most beautiful cafés in the country. Judi's art is everywhere — from the permanent counter front to the regularly changing wall art.

Judi works in the studio attached to her shop — the hot-ticket item when we are there are some glorious ceramic creations of lingerie and women's outer clothing.

The café made its name as one of the Lonely Planet's top ten cafés in New Zealand, and the word has spread with turnover continually increasing. Andrew and Jo have made it their mission to live up to the hype, providing excellence in food, coffee and service. At one point they were working seven days a week and became exhausted without making any gains for their effort expended. They employed a business coach, and have the evangelical fervour of the converted relating how this has improved both the business and their lifestyle.

**The café is a treat for both the eye and the palate.** Some of the food is staple in the cabinet, with regulars enjoying coming back to enjoy their favourite treat consistently, but flanking the staples are seasonal goodies. Andrew and Jo pride themselves on innovation; you won't find a panini, scone or muffin on the premises.

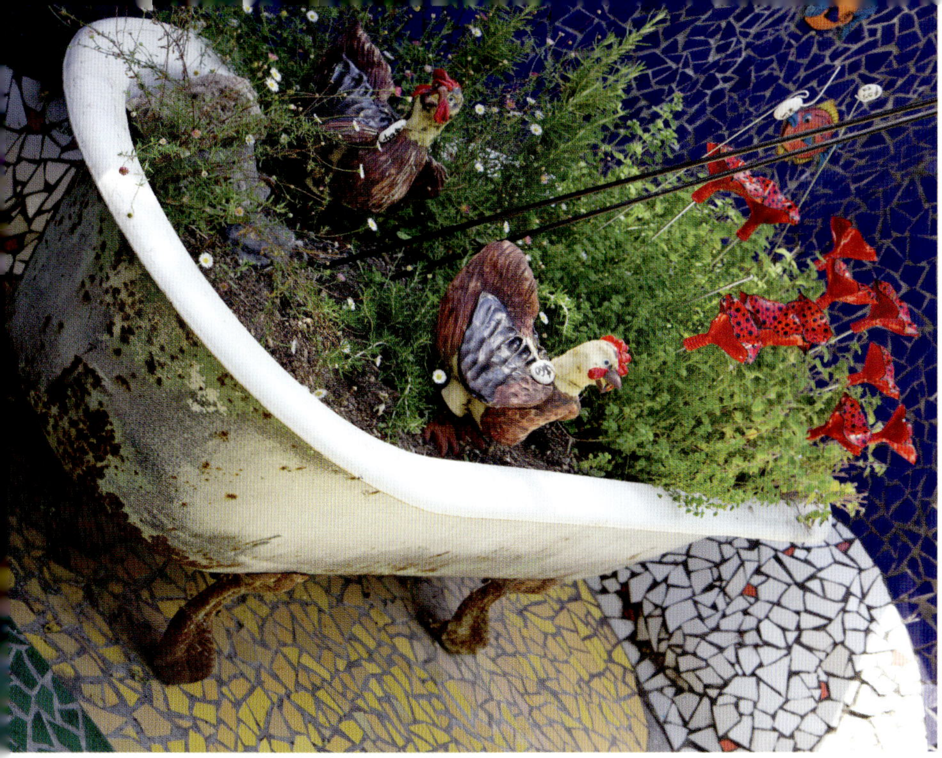

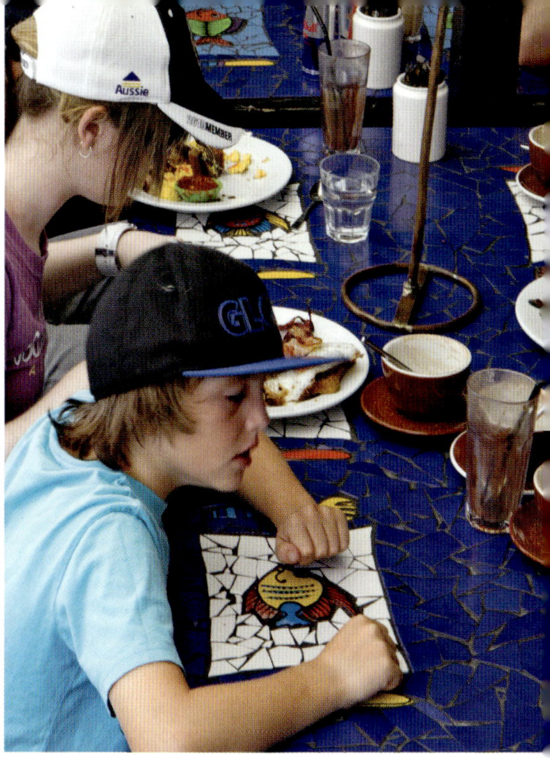
Aussie

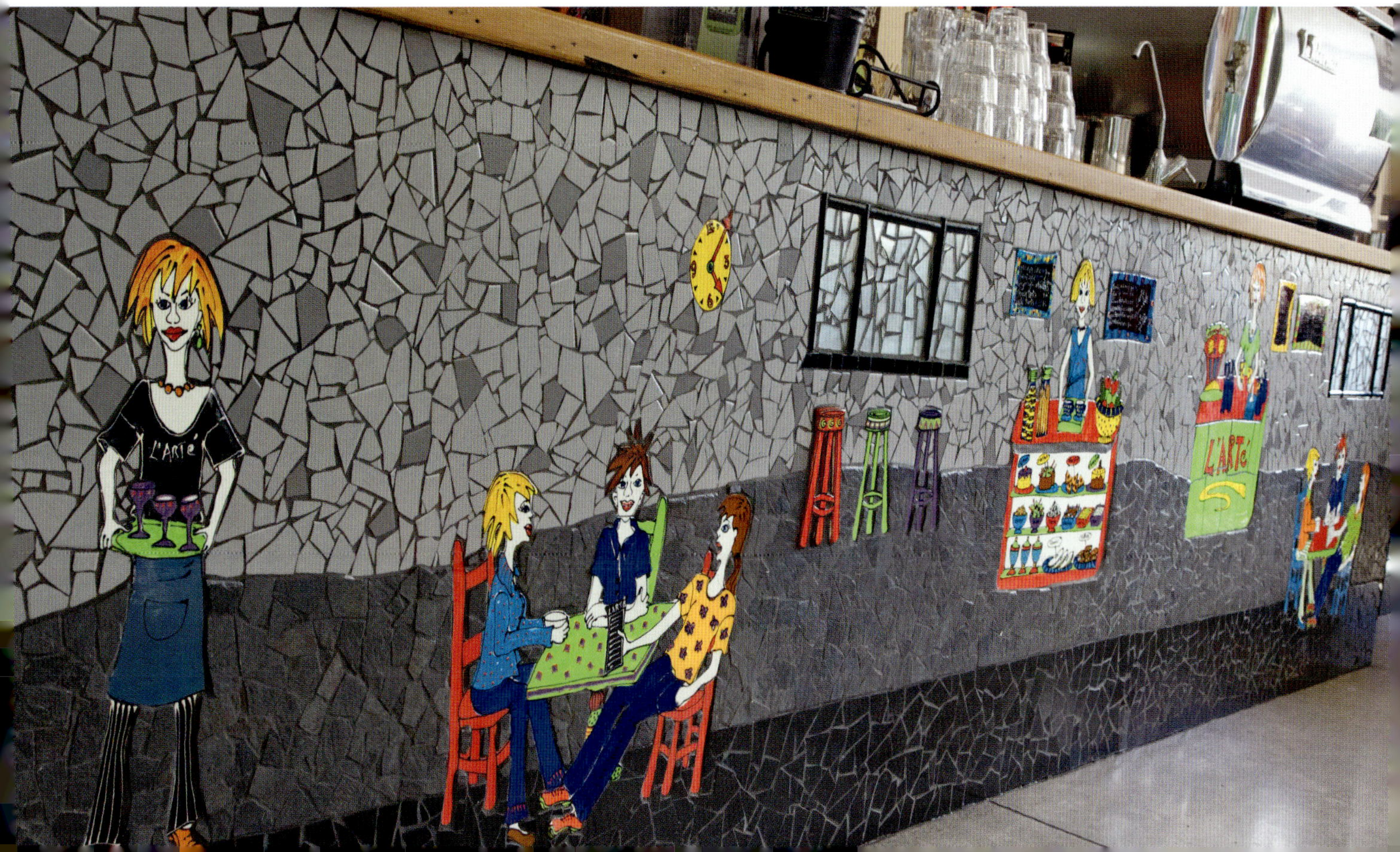
L'ARTé
L'ARTé

From Taupo we head to the coast again; this time it's the Coromandel, via a café we heard of in Arapuni. It's supposed to be by a dam, and neither of us has any idea of what the place or area is like.

# RHUBARB CAFÉ

**6 Arapuni Road**
**ARAPUNI**

### ROCKET

Is rhubarb a vegetable or a fruit? Whatever, it is undervalued as a yummy sweet treat. One of Matthew's best memories is of rhubarb crumble and Niki still thinks you can't beat it with thick Greek yoghurt and homemade muesli. So when we walk into Bryan and Louise Samuel's café Rhubarb, and Phoebe Snow is playing on the stereo, **it is a meeting of two of her favourite good feelings: old home kitchens and great music. She is sold.**

Louise is an education police officer Monday to Friday; Bryan spent 25 years as a breakdown shift fitter at a plywood mill up until 2010 when he came in to do the café. His skills are pretty good in his new-found passion, and he makes beautiful coffee. Louise came across Bryan while spending time in Tokoroa, he took her fancy and she decided she wanted him. Three months after meeting they got together, and four years later they are still going strong. Their long-term plans are to change their lifestyle, with Louise hoping to give up her day job for the business full time.

Louise and Bryan's priority when they opened was to provide something special for the locals, and they in return have shown great support. With a population of only 350, everyone knows each other and a bit of old-time New Zealand community still exists.

One of the exciting advances in the area is the bike trail that is part of the national one linking the whole country, and a welcome addition to the existing and expanding walkways in the area. While we are at Rhubarb a group of eight red-faced walkers arrive for their treat at the end of the trail. They'd left Auckland at 6 am, walked up and around the river and are back in time for lunch — not a bad way to spend a Sunday morning.

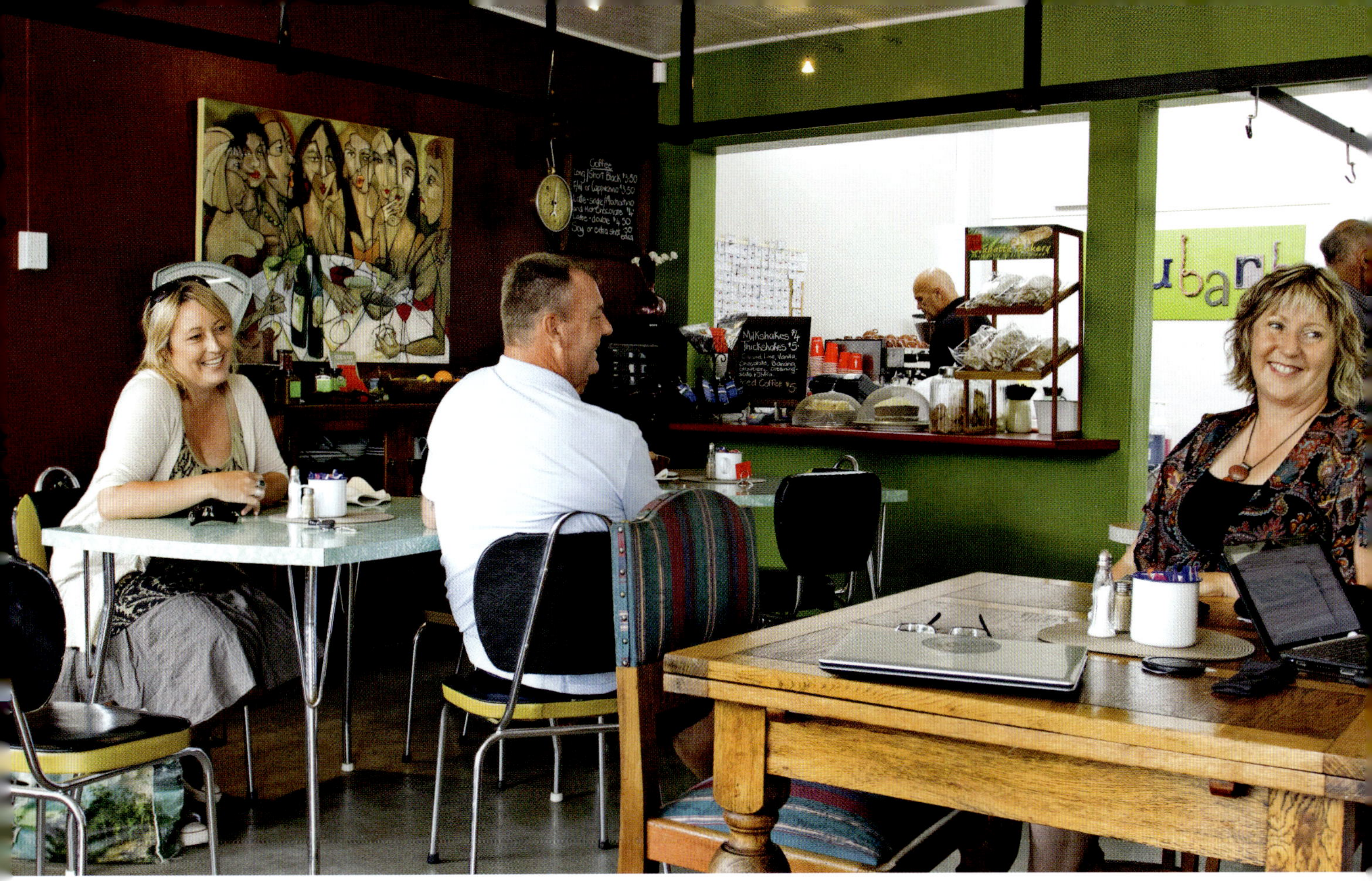

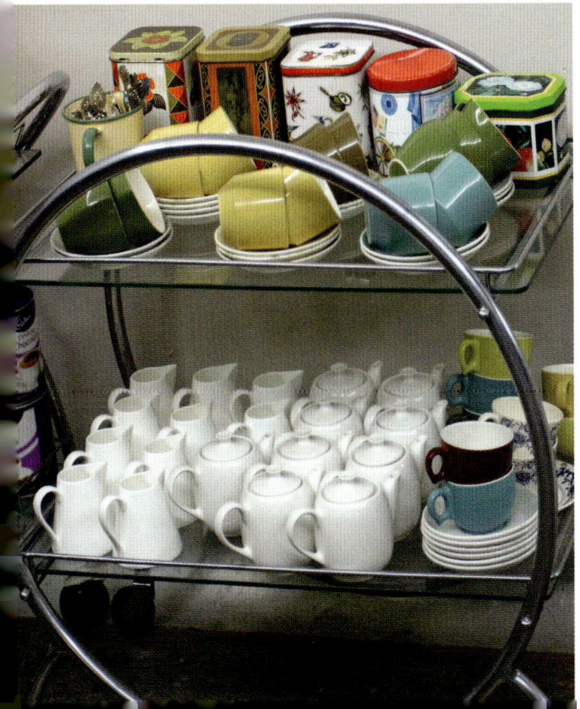

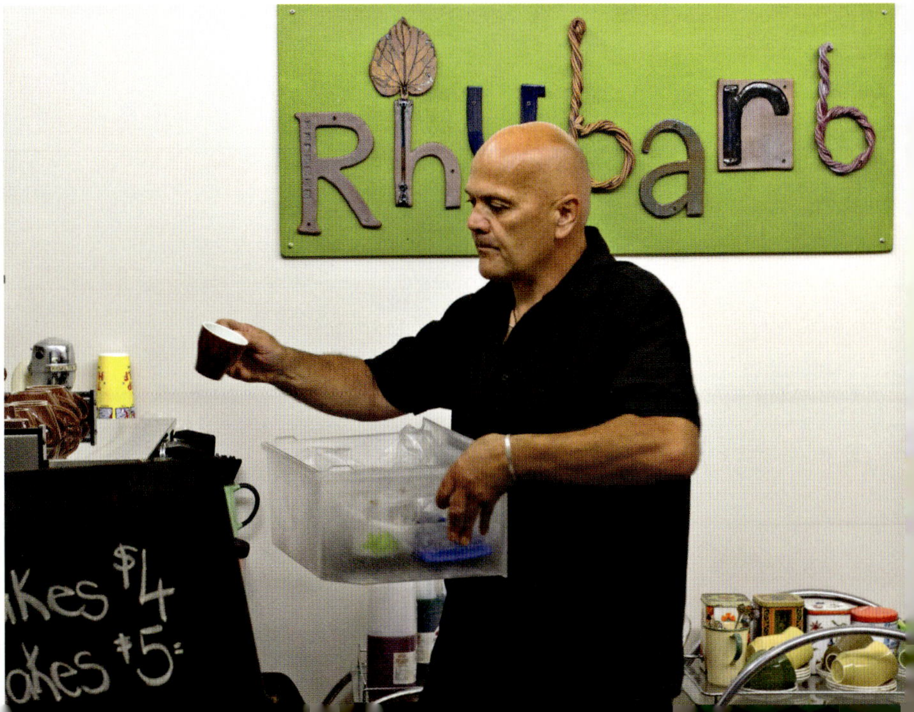
Rhubarb
akes $4
akes $5:

By the time we reach the goldmine town of Waihi, we are in need of a coffee and a swim. The Coromandel is known for its beautiful beaches; we reckon Waihi has some of the best. We don't stop in the town but head straight to the beach and the Flatwhite Café. A swim in the surf gets us knocked over, repeatedly, and clears away the grumpy feelings we have. Now it's time for coffee.

# FLATWHITE BEACHFRONT CAFÉ

**21 Shaw Road**
**WAIHI BEACH**

### KARAJOZ

In March 2005 Andy Kennedy bought an underdeveloped café called Flatwhite. He arrived on a beautiful day, looked at the view and thought, 'You don't often get spots like this in New Zealand, close to the water, etc.' Within a month of looking at the café he had purchased it. Andy's premise was that with the right offerings people will come; and they do come, 364 days a year for breakfast, lunch and dinner. When Andy first came here all the cafés closed in the early afternoon and on Sunday, Monday and Tuesday. He figured he could tap into the three local campgrounds and be consistently open.

The food philosophy was established early on — cover all the bases and have something that would appeal to all who walked in. He does this with ice cream, pizza, all-day brunch and a great dinner menu to choose from. The café is also licensed. This approach has been rewarded with returning customers, and one who even emailed to let Andy know that in an 18-month world tour the best breakfast consumed was at Flatwhite. Andy is chuffed by that.

The building can handle sand and rowdy kids, although the threat of duct tape available for the restraining of said kids may keep the energy levels down. **This place really is family-, beach-, and kid-friendly;** it doesn't matter if the kids spill things. And the word is that many a celebrity holiday-home owner frequents the café, so you can do your part-time paparazzi work while soaking up the rays and enjoying your coffee.

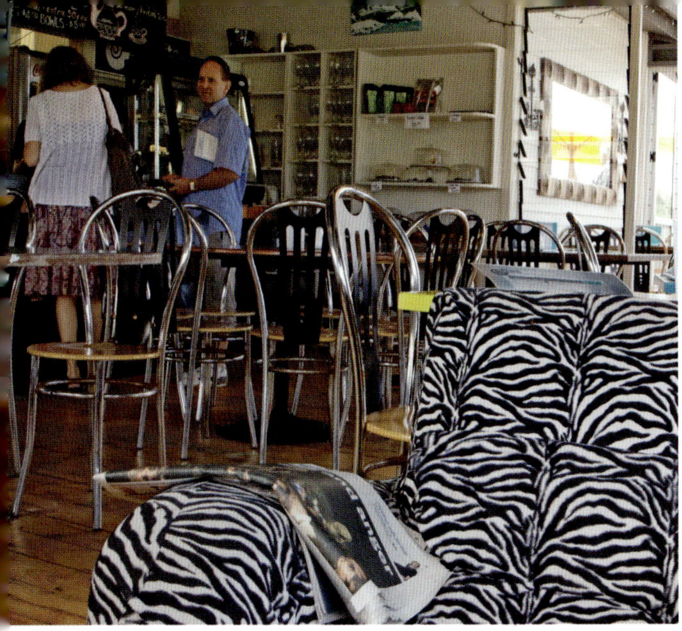

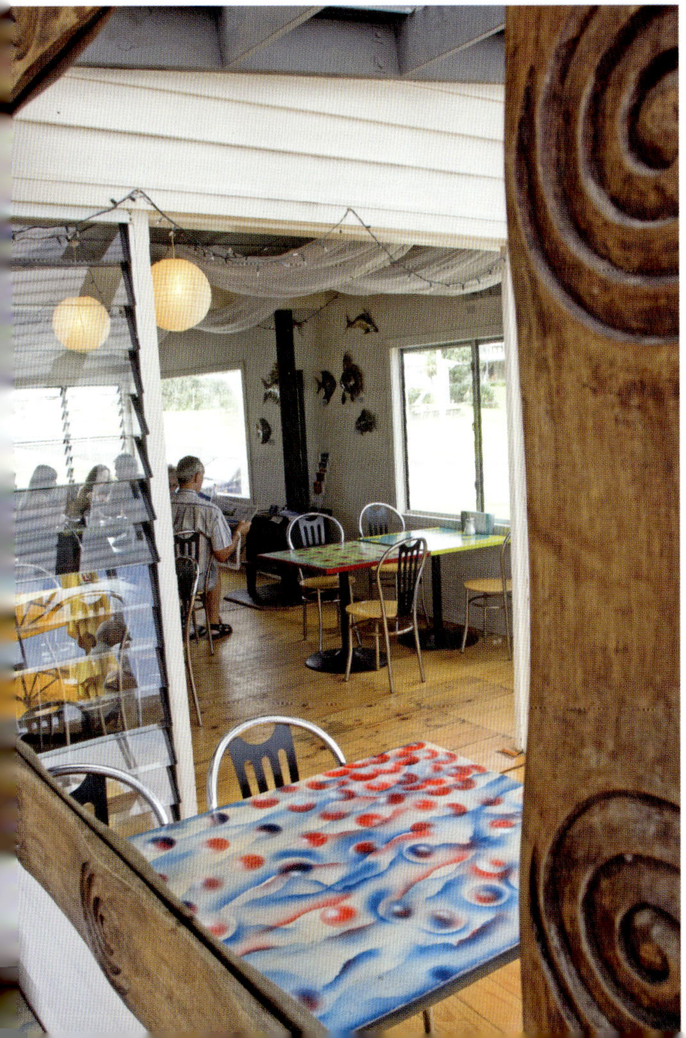

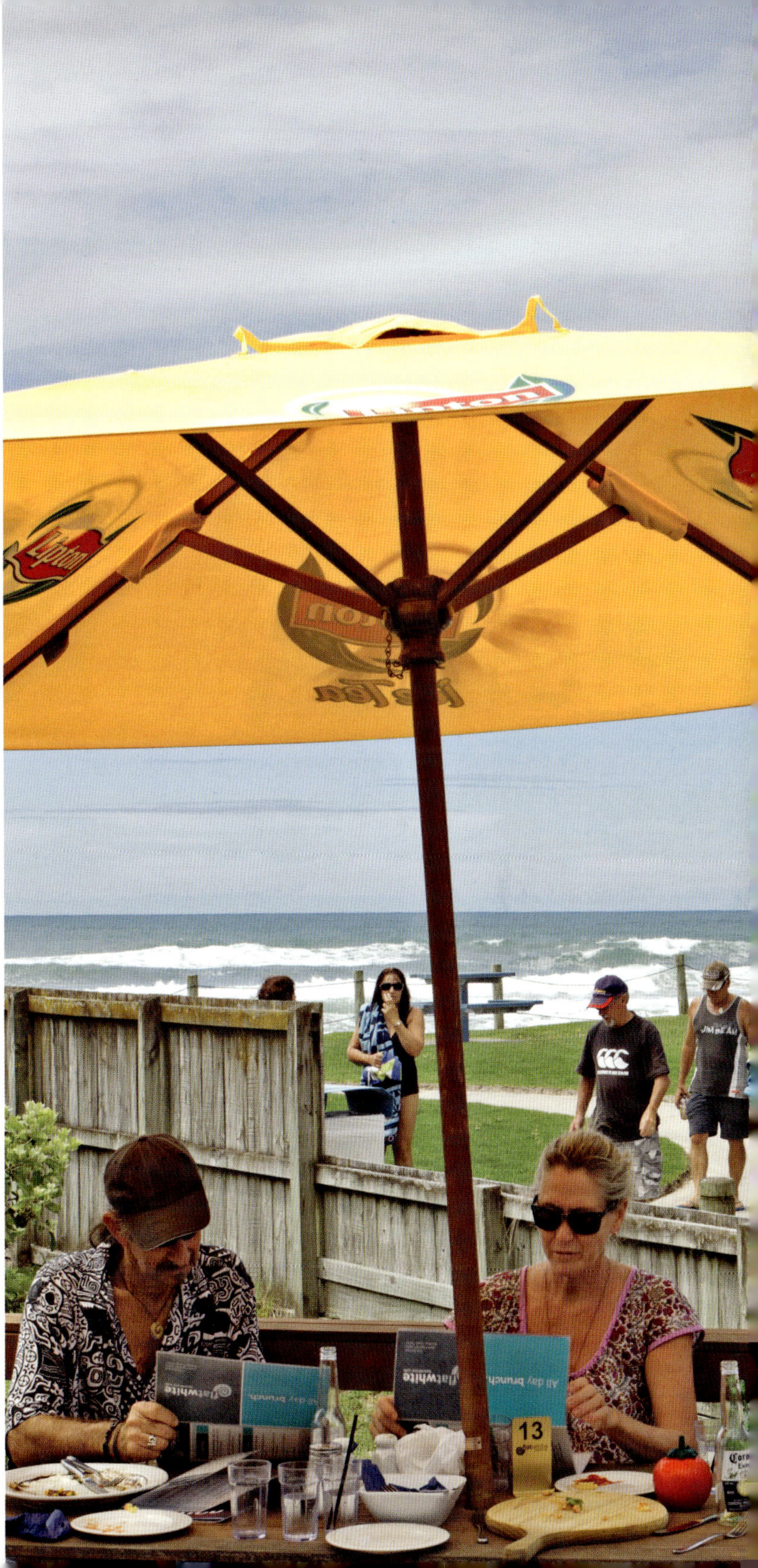
All day brunch.
13

Matthew has an image of Whangamata as the town that everyone gets drunk in over New Year. At least that is how he remembers it as a teenager. It's a little more refined now, but it is still at its busiest in the summer, with many houses empty for the other seasons. We drive around reminiscing on our childhood experiences and notice a café almost on the beach. Ah, this is the place with the famous Mongrel Dog, we think. And next morning we are back to try it.

# BLACKIES ON THE BEACH

**418 Ocean Road, Williamson Park**
**WHANGAMATA**

### GRAVITY

Some cafés rise up to supply the demand that occurs in the summer months, and Blackies is a perfect example of this. Owned by Dee and Bryan Black, who live elsewhere but have strong affiliations with the Whangamata Surf Club, the café is run by managers from October through to April.

Blackies is in the perfect location to make use of and accommodate the thousands of beachgoers who descend upon Whangamata in summer. Being situated right beside the surf club and public amenities makes it a place that most will come into contact with. **To complement the perfect location they have food that is right on target, too.** There is a full menu including a nippers section (young surfer) for the kids, breakfast and pizza. The food we try is made by the chef of the moment — John Barke.

Bryan and Dee Black have been hands-on with the creation of what is now in place. Bryan was committed to sourcing local produce where possible and spent time with John looking around to find the best. So here you have local produce made by an imported chef at one of New Zealand's iconic beach destinations — what a great combo. We have been recommended the Mongrel Dog, which includes sausage made by a local butcher and is perfect for the hunger that comes from playing in the surf for hours, most impressive.

As we try the Mongrel Dog one of the locals suggests that an even better option is the Salt and Pepper Squid. Never ones to turn down food while working in cafés (waistline expanding daily) we do. WOW . . . we have been travelling for nearly three months and this food from a pop-up café on the beach is up there with the best we have tried.

# BLACKIES ON THE BEACH'S SALT & PEPPER SQUID

### SQUID DUST
- ½ teaspoon ground white pepper
- ½ teaspoon ground black pepper
- ½ teaspoon ground cayenne pepper
- ½ teaspoon lemon pepper
- ½ teaspoon schezuan pepper
- 2 teaspoons salt
- 3 teaspoons polenta, fine
- 3 teaspoons flour

### CASHEW NUT SAMBAL
- 1 cup raw unsalted cashew nuts
- 1 ½ cups desiccated coconut
- ¾ cup white sesame seeds
- ¾ cup black sesame seeds
- ½ cup sweet chilli sauce
- ½ cup sweet soy sauce

### DRESSING
- ¼ cup sesame oil
- ¼ cup olive oil
- ¼ cup soya bean oil
- juice and zest of 3 limes
- 1 sprig coriander (leaves, stem, roots and all)
- thumb-size piece of unpeeled ginger
- 3 cloves garlic
- ½ cup sweet chilli sauce
- ¼ cup soy sauce
- ¼ cup sweet soy sauce

Preheat oven to 160°C. Mix the squid dust ingredients together, it should be an orange earthy colour.

Combine first four ingredients of sambal and roast, stirring every 5 minutes or so. Once the mix has a lightly roasted brown appearance remove from oven and leave to cool. Combine roasted mix with sweet chilli sauce and sweet soy sauce.

For the dressing, combine the first three oils and set aside. Blend remaining ingredients and slowly drizzle in the oil mixture.

Gently toss together two portions mesclun, three sliced spring onions and one cup of the sambal.

Cut four squid tubes in your favourite style. Roll the squid in the squid dust. Heat oil in a pan (hot but not smoking) and gently add squid. After 15 seconds turn and cook for a further 15 seconds.

Drain on a paper towel, being careful not to dislodge the coating. Arrange squid on plates and place a generous amount of salad on top. Add dressing to taste and serve with a wedge of lime.

Serves two.

We leave Whangamata and head further up the Coromandel towards the world famous Hot Water beach, named because you can swim in the surf (cold water), or when the tide is just right dig a big hole in the sand and make a spa (hot water). We spend some time at the beach before our next stop — a place we had not visited for a very long time.

# COLENSO

### Tairua Whitianga Road, State Highway 25
### WHENUAKITE

### ATOMIC

From humble beginnings often great things can come. Colenso is an example of one idea becoming another bigger and brighter one. More than two decades on from growing fruit on the peninsula, the owners of Colenso café have created one of the area's classic places to visit, regularly as a local and as a must-do for visitors to the area.

Ruth and Andy Pettitt planted the land as orchards. Struggling to make ends meet they investigated producing juice. In order to juice they needed a commercial kitchen; once that was there it seemed sensible to create a small café and so Colenso came into being. As the longevity of the business suggests, a café was the right choice; the orchards are now very much in the back seat.

In the beginning the wonderful gardens were non-existent; money was short so herb cuttings and plants were often donations or garden centre sale items. Ruth has made the garden her project, along with her faithful hardworking staff. These days the gardens are beautiful — there is a playground for children and shaded areas behind the café to sit and enjoy the food and coffee. **Drinking coffee in this peaceful, natural setting is a must as a restorative for the soul.** Eating food that is grown in that same setting has a similar benefit for the body. Every plate goes out with at least a garnish from the garden, and generally the substance of what is on your plate is local.

Once your soul and body have been taken care of, you can get on with replenishing your cupboards with items of beauty and taste. The shop in the café has jewellery, homeware, preserves, hats, cards and more, to tempt and allow you to take away a memory.

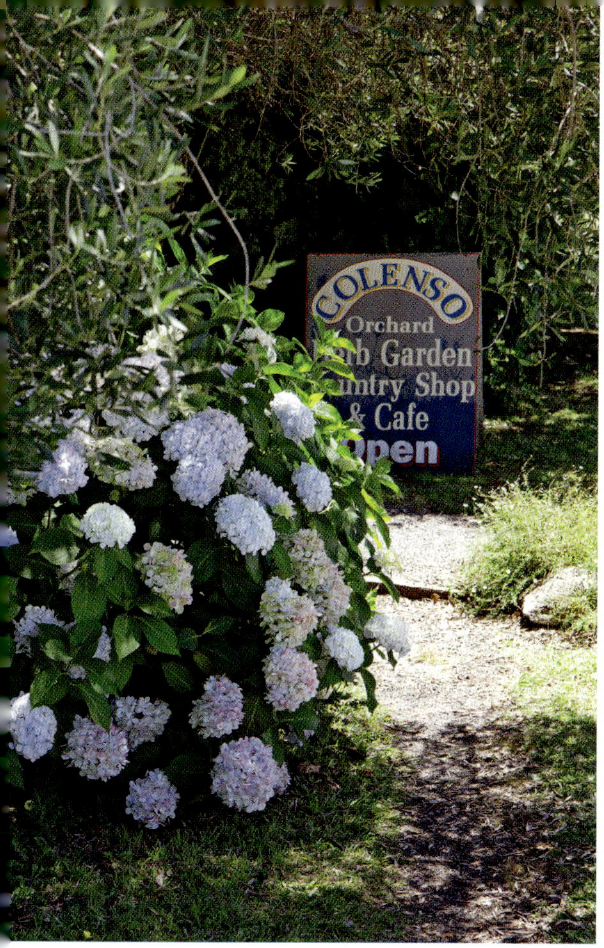
COLENSO
Orchard
Garden
Shop
Cafe

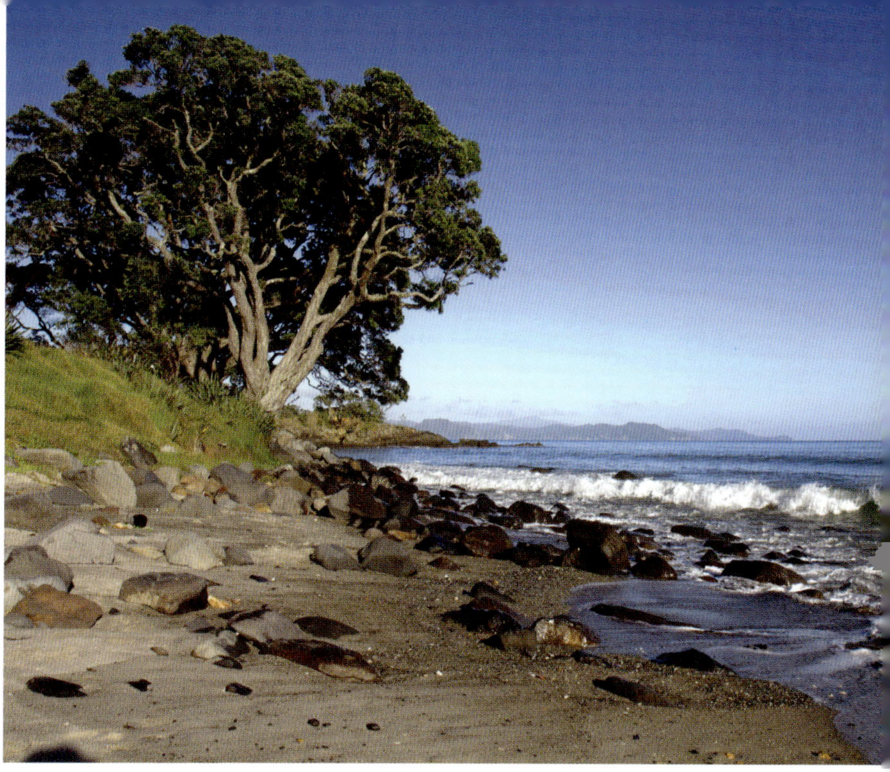

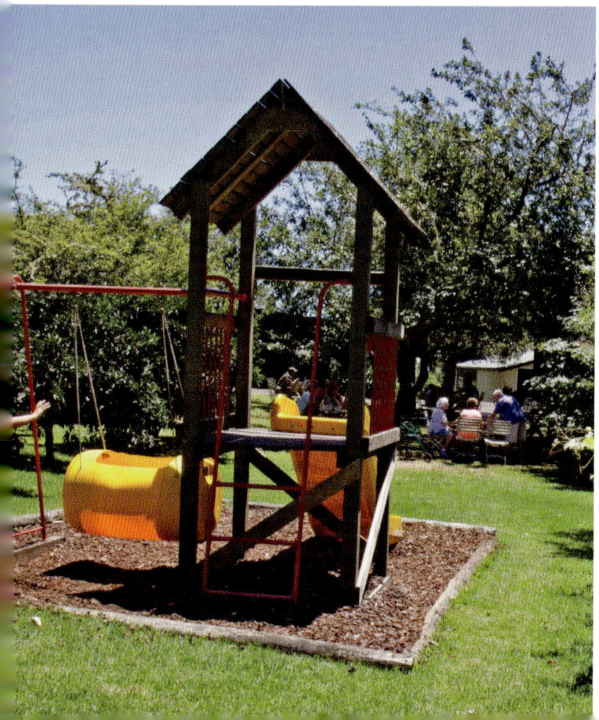

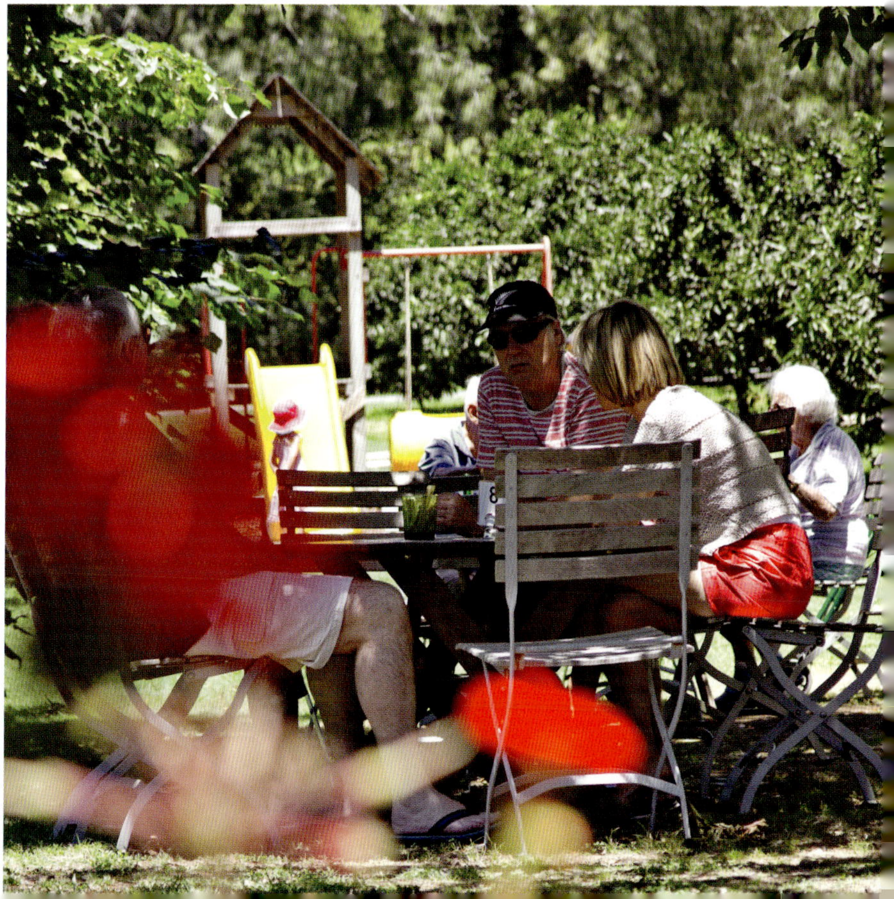

Before we head over the hills to Coromandel town, we find a little bay and quite by chance a café. We drive across a small bridge and enter the pizza world of Luke's Kitchen. We swim, eat, drink coffee and chat to an ever-increasing number of locals who arrive at the end of the day to feast.

# LUKE'S KITCHEN — BLACKJACK ART GALLERY AND CAFÉ

20 Blackjack Road, Kuaotunu, RD2
WHITIANGA

### COFFEE LALA

This is our new favourite place to be on the Coromandel Peninsula, Kuaotunu. Once we have enjoyed a coffee from Blackjack we go back to Luke's Kitchen. Luke starts chatting to us about his place and then incrementally the place gets busier and busier until he is unable to talk and his dad takes over. We discover this is how these businesses work too, by overlapping.

Paul Riley is the beginning of the story. He used to come to Kuaotunu on holiday as a child from Auckland. Around 1980 he came back to the area to live. He was the local motor mechanic and his workshop was in the building that now houses the gallery/espresso outlet. Slowly the batteries and oil moved out the back door as the espresso machine and art rolled in the front door, until the transformation to art gallery and café was complete.

Luke has been working in kitchens from around 14 years old, earning money to spend on his love of surfing. He trained as a chef, then spent a number of winters travelling to Samoa, Queenstown and Perth pursuing his foodie passion. A few years ago Luke, with the help of Paul, created Luke's Kitchen.

Word has spread and now the summers are insanely busy, resulting in Luke becoming completely shattered by the end of the season. Despite this, Luke is able to greet all with enthusiasm. In 2011 the kitchen will be open for its first winter season, with one of Luke's friends carrying the torch while Luke takes his traditional time away. **Here you will find music on occasion, sunsets daily, great wood-fired pizza, excellent coffee and a tight-knit community. Top it all off with a swim in the warm water; life doesn't get much better than this.**

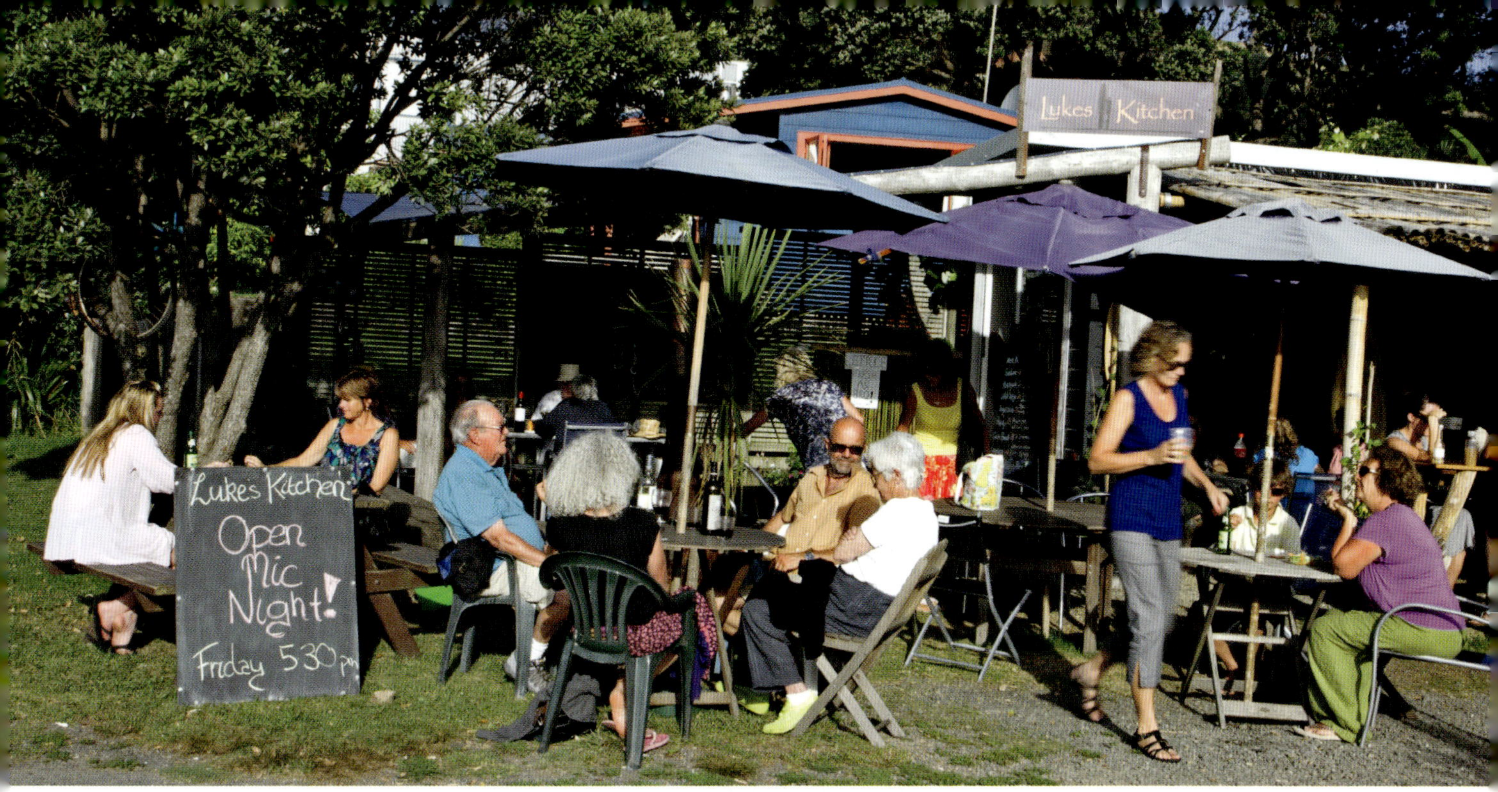
Lukes Kitchen
Lukes Kitchen
Open
Mic
Night!
Friday 530pm

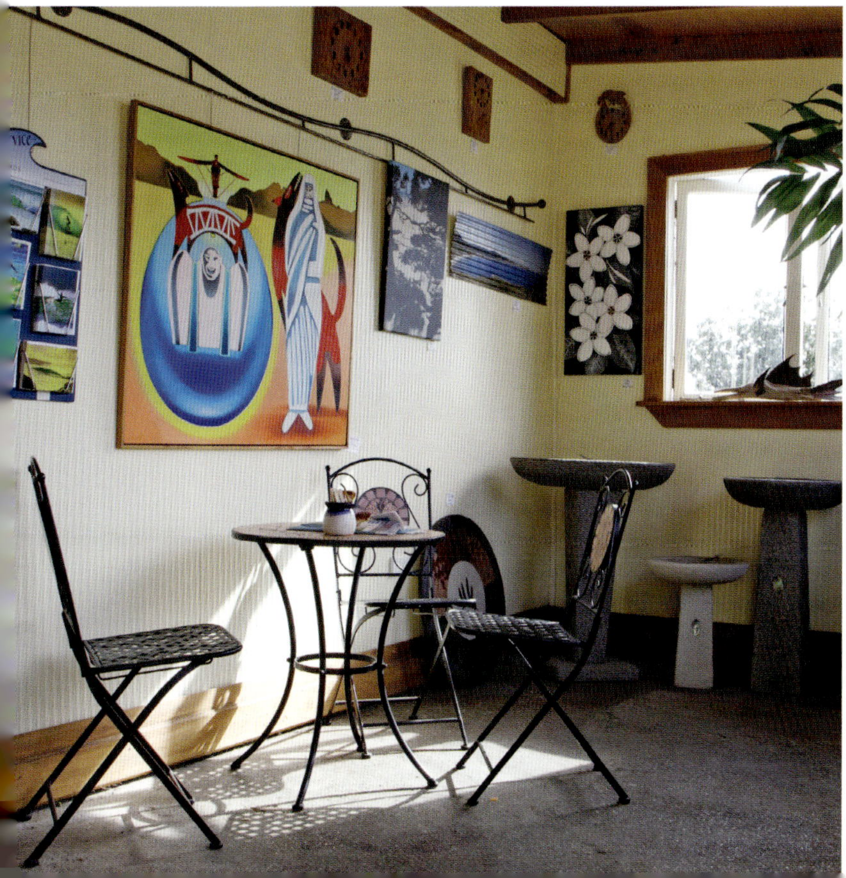

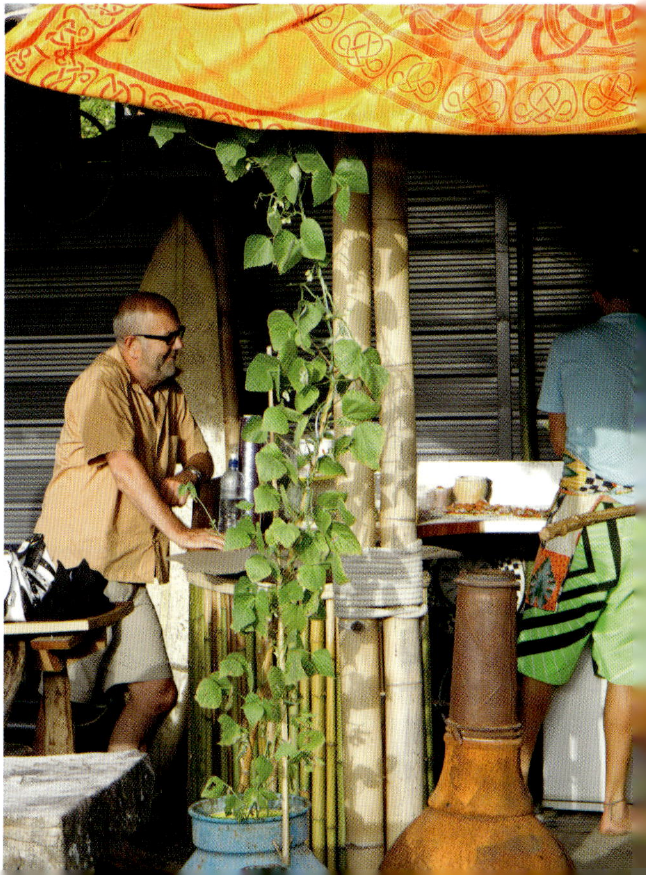

It is late in the day as we go over the hills to Coromandel town. We arrive at our next place to stay, a lovely old New Orleans-style villa. Coromandel town has a pace that you will never get in the city. The rhythm is more natural and you can feel your soul being rejuvenated. Our next café provides exactly this, and a sense of calm befalls us.

# DRIVING CREEK CAFÉ

**180 Driving Creek Road
COROMANDEL TOWN**

## COFFEE LALA

Driving Creek Café has the best French toast we have ever tried . . . no exceptions . . . but, sadly, we do not have the recipe to pass on. Cinnamon and berries play a part in the creation — you just have to go and try it out.

This café was set up by Bryce Stevens to complement the Driving Creek Railway just a little further up the road. He was a potter in the winter and ran the café in the summer months. The land is owned by a trust and although the café was originally communally driven, it is now owned by Michal and Jessica Dziwulski. Jessica came to Coromandel in years gone by and knew that at some point she would return to live. When the café became available her dream was realised and the couple made their life here in 2005.

**The stereotypical vibe of the Coromandel is captured in this café. The food is organic where possible and covertly vegetarian.** Driving Creek Café has managed to put together a menu that appeals to all, quietly leaving out the meat; very clever. When we arrive there is a real variety of people enjoying the bush setting, so although this place could be seen as alternative it is mainstream friendly. It is also dog and child friendly, with a great play area within eyesight of the covered outdoor seating.

Michal is currently the hands-on member of the partnership as Jessica looks after their two children. He has created a second-hand bookshop within the café and has plans to expand it, and we like it.

The other aspect we really like is the pottery created in the style of Bryce Stevens by local artist Petra Meyboden, which your food and coffee is served in and on. It is a welcome change to the standard crockery elsewhere, a celebration of differences in style and essence.

Love &

Maple Syrup, & Berry Compote
French Toast – Thick Cut w/ Creme Fraiche,
Grilled Cinnamon Pears, & Berry Coulis $15.50
Scrambled Free Range Eggs w/ Roast Potatos
Chutney, Wilted Greens, & Chunky Toast $16.50
Omelette – Free Range Eggs w/ Sundried
Tomato Pesto, Parmesan, & Spinach on Toast $16.50
Scrambled Organic Tofu in a Seasoned Sauce w/
Roast Potatos, Chutney, & Greens on Toast $17.50
Dhal – Mildly Spiced
Nachos – Bean & Organ
Savoury Crepes w/
Tofu Burger – Organic
Salad Creations –
Breakfast – All Day –
Gluten Free Toast $2.00

From Coromandel we head through Auckland to the far north. By the time we reach our next character café we need a decent stop and time to recuperate. The café before Helena Bay on the east coast is the perfect place.

# THE CAFÉ HELENA BAY HILL

**1392 Old Russell Road, RD4**
**HIKURANGI**

## ATOMIC

In December 2003 Peter Brown opened an art gallery and gardens on the hill on the way down to Helena Bay. He is still there with 20,000 or so people coming through the doors annually. Two weeks after he opened a couple of German tourists walked through those doors. Uwe Krohmann and Julia Nuechter were travelling around the country, Julia for the second time. Immediately there was a rapport and Uwe and Julia began to think about coming back to the area.

They continued travelling for six months and went back to Germany with the thought that if they were dissatisfied in Europe they would return to New Zealand. They did return and tried their luck with Peter Brown, hoping to start a café with a view that is arguably unrivalled. After some discussion the deal was done and the building began. The café opened Labour weekend 2005.

**The first thing that strikes us on arriving in the café is the view out over the native bush and Helena Bay — it is very special and available from most seats in the café.** The next thing is the welcoming manner of Julia who has a real passion for hospitality. Although the café is off the main highway north, it services many holiday homes and the regular visitors to the area are often regulars at the café.

Food at Helena Bay is standard Kiwi food with a European twist. They serve German bread on the breakfast menu and while many of the cakes may not be as sweet as we are used to, they are still delicious.

The bonus to enjoying the café is that directly next door you can also enjoy the gallery that stocks local and national art works. We discover that it is possible to spend a minimal amount in the gallery and take home just a little something, and there is opportunity for those who are able to buy the signature statement; either way there is much to look at and enjoy.

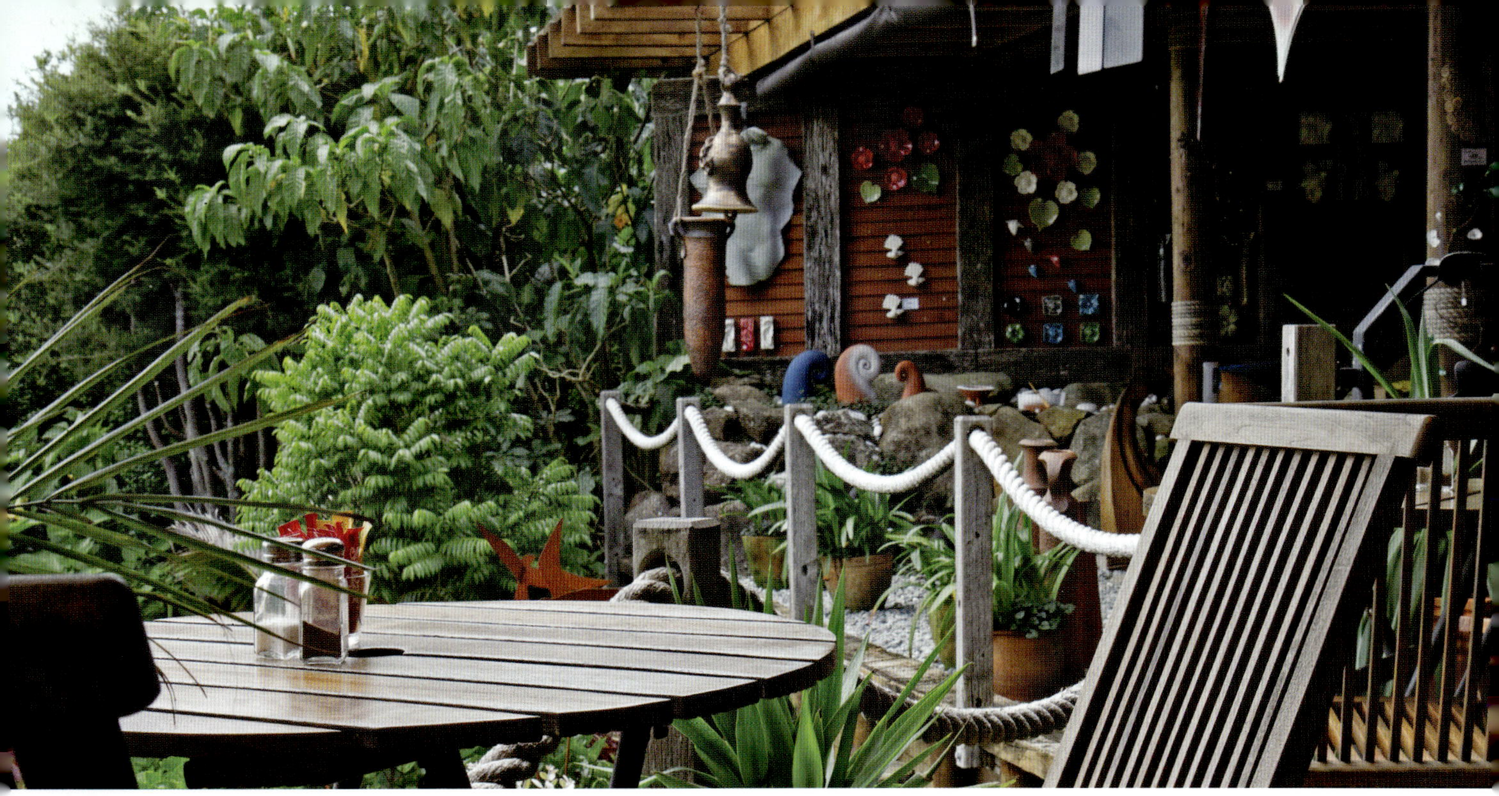

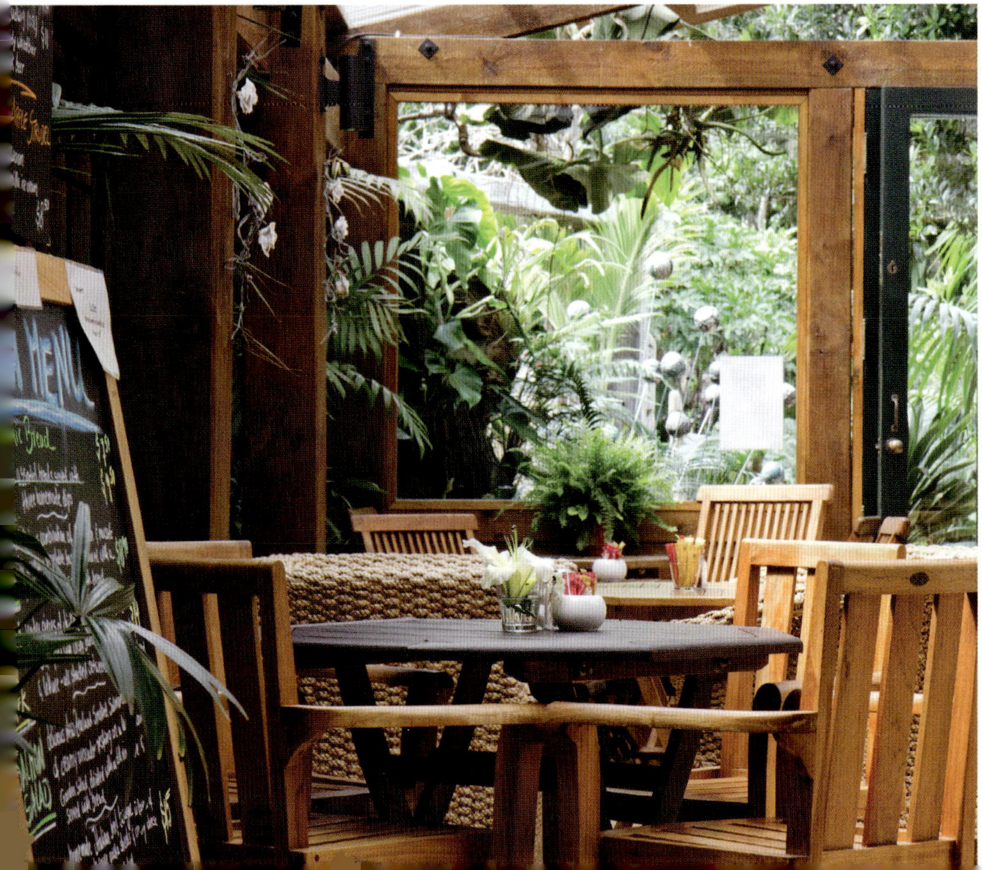

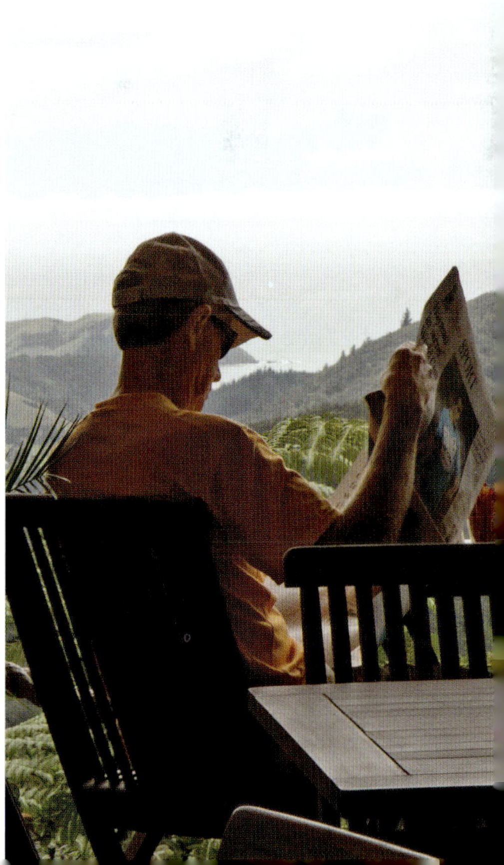

Take the time to go off the main drag; it's not a huge detour and after enjoying a drink, make your way down to the beach for a walk or swim. The Kiwi life is a good one. It is a couple of hours before we leave and, feeling rested, decide to drive all the way to Kerikeri. As night falls we settle into the Kerikeri Court Motel. Next morning, we head off to Rawene to explore the Boatshed Café.

# BOATSHED CAFÉ

**8 Clendon Esplanade**
**RAWENE**

**ALLPRESS**

Tucked away in an album at home we have a photo of Mika, Ruby and good friend Trudi on the deck at the Boatshed Café. The kids were much smaller than they are now, and Niki had blonde hair; thankfully things have changed for the better. But the Boatshed Café has stayed the same, **an internationally known café in a small, remote part of New Zealand that consistently delivers simple good food and excellent coffee.**

Craig and Kirsty Joiner came to the Hokianga from Wellington in 1973 with their four children. Craig was a builder and able to find work in his trade and then on to varying occupations to keep supporting the family in this work-sparse area. Eventually they began a yacht charter business in conjunction with the café. The café took off and the charter business didn't. Nearly two decades later the Joiners are still here, although when we visit the café is for sale and when it does sell Craig hopes to continue working in the business. The formula has worked for a long time, so new owners would do well to keep on the same track.

One of the really appealing things about this café is its location. Rawene is a town renowned for talented artists and musicians. There is a special quality that comes from being on the Hokianga Harbour and this café really *is* on the harbour with the water flowing under the building. Should you be so inclined, it would be possible to catch a fish while enjoying your flat white.

One of the benefits of being around for a long time is the connection with the community that develops. Many local teenage girls have worked in the café, starting on dishes and being trained up to be able to handle cooking the full menu. Some of those may have gone on to become mothers of new café workers . . . the wheel just keeps turning.

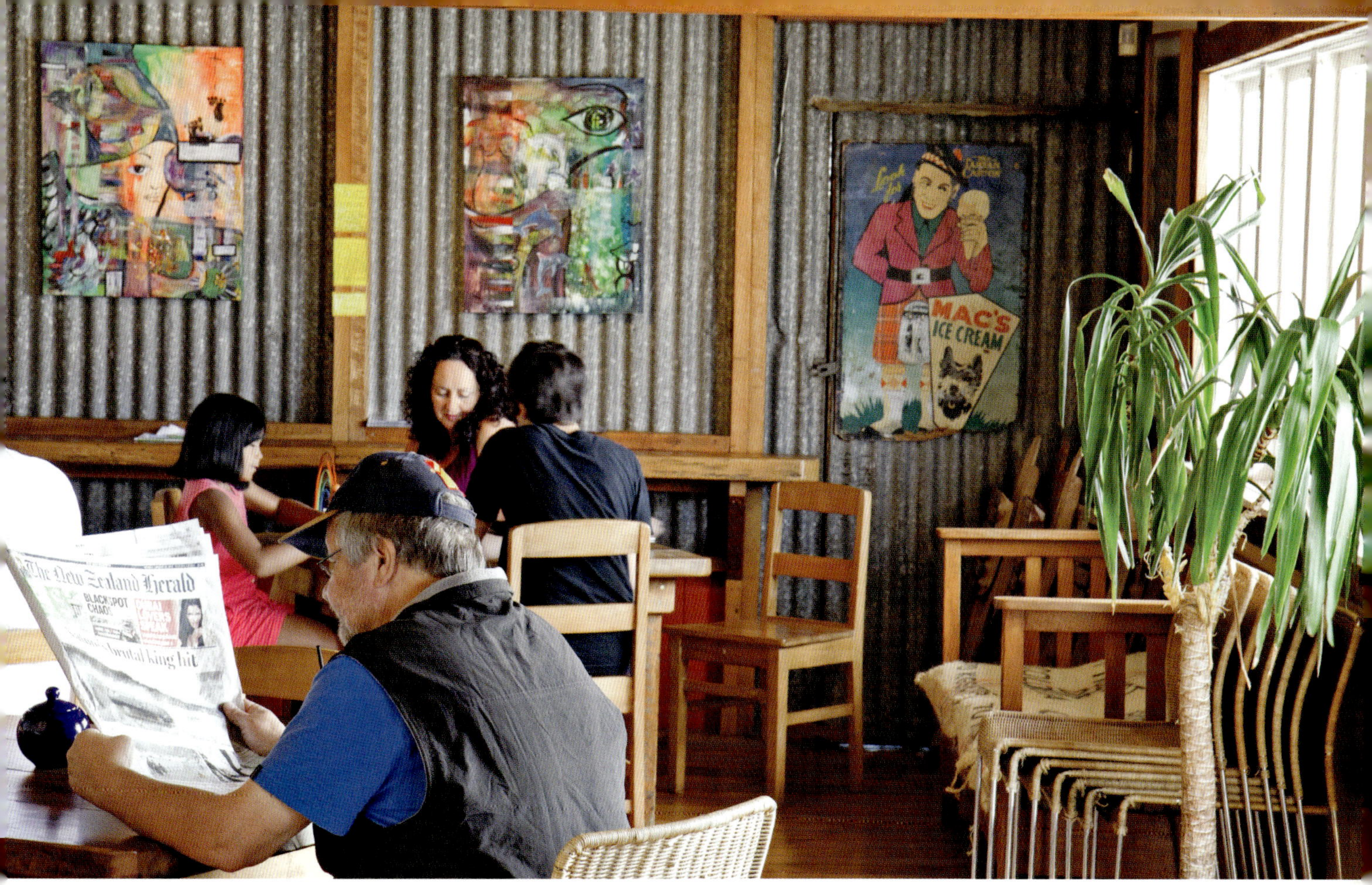
The New Zealand Herald
MAC'S ICE CREAM

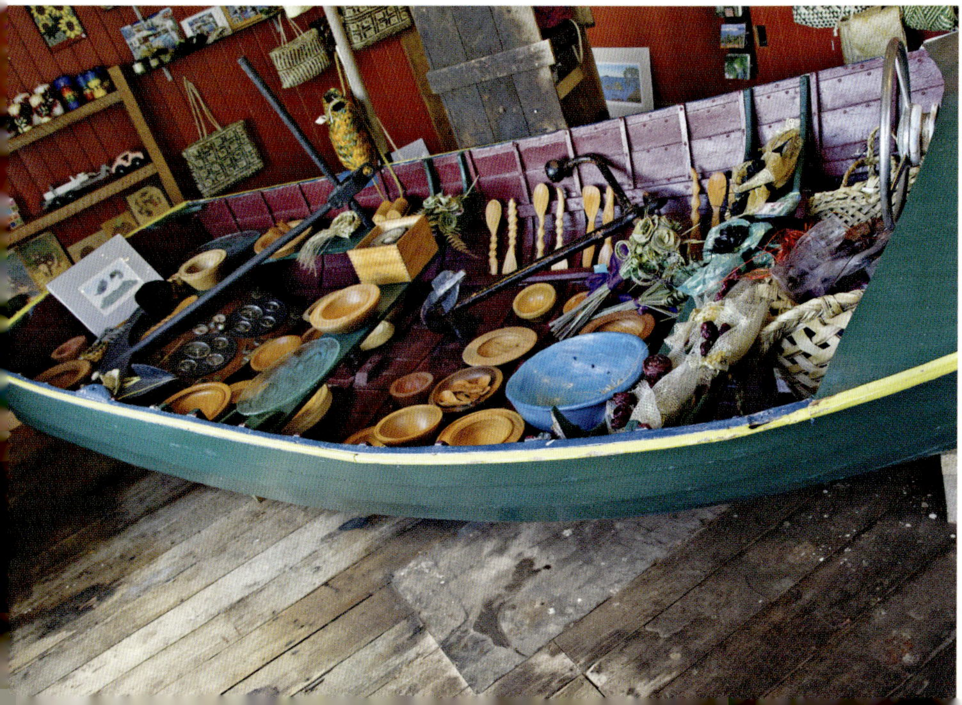

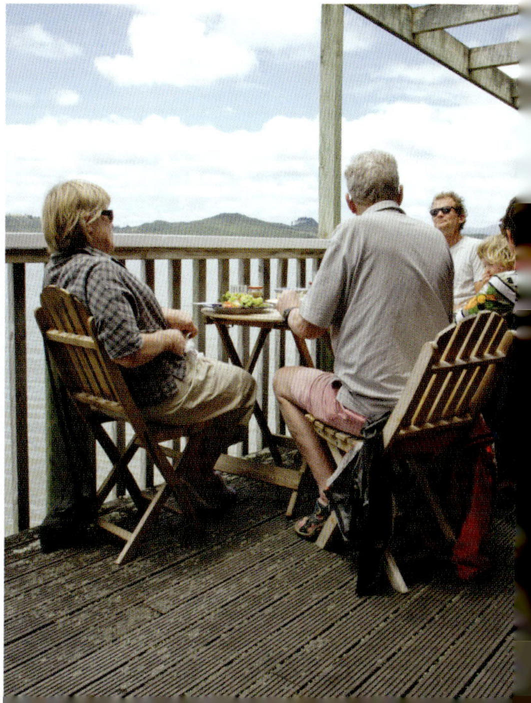

For our next stop we head to the tropics and our next café. It's on the way down to the Stone Store at Kerikeri, a well-known tourist attraction.

# FOOD AT WHAREPUKE

**Wharepuke Subtropical Garden, 190 Kerikeri Road
KERIKERI**

### KARAJOZ

As we drive down the driveway the subtropical aspect becomes clear with the gardens oozing forward to meet you. This is the beginning of the experience. Up the wooden pathway with a step to the left and into the café you go. During the day this is a café with a casual feel, there is cabinet food and a menu to choose from. The style is Thai, but if that isn't your thing you will still be able to eat with pleasure. In the evenings things become a little more upmarket and generally on a Friday night you can join a Thai banquet.

**Food at Wharepuke is near the top, if not the top, of the list regarding excellence in all areas.** Colin Ashton is the owner/chef along with his wife Rachael Goldfinch who works front of house. Colin originates from Wales where he grew up in his parents' restaurant and cultivated his love of creating food. He has gone on tour as chef with Shania Twain and the Red Hot Chilli Peppers and has brought all of his skill and passion for food into his own place in Kerikeri.

The food is the big drawcard here; everything is created by Colin with precision and dedication. Tasting his food is simply sublime, and the wonderful bonus is that he and Rachael are nice people too. If you are lucky Rachael won't be too busy and you will get a chance to have a chat. She is the sort of woman who, after two meetings, was giving us hugs on the way out.

Both Rachael and Colin's parents have moved to Kerikeri to work in the business and be with the couple's three children. The workload is shared out, with the only constant being Colin in the kitchen whenever the café is open, which is every day except Sunday night and all day Monday.

In case you haven't already gathered, we have a wonderful time at Food at Wharepuke. We meet some great people and eat some astounding food. We will be back.

# FOOD AT WHAREPUKE'S PORK BELLY

200g pork belly (Freedom Farms is best)
1 cup light soy sauce
1 piece ginger, sliced
1 cup chicken stock
4 cups water
1 stick lemongrass
2 kaffir lime leaves
2 whole star anise
2 cinnamon sticks
3 cloves garlic whole

**DRESSING**
2 cloves garlic
2 green Thai chillies
2 cm piece ginger root (grated)
½ cup light soy sauce
½ cup thick sweet soy sauce
½ cup rice vinegar
½ cup caster sugar
½ cup tamarind puree

Preheat oven to 160°C. Combine all ingredients apart from pork. Place pork belly in a small tray not much bigger than the belly, and cover with remaining ingredients. Cover with foil, tightly seal and braise in the oven for 2 ½ to 3 hours, until very tender. Take out of braising stock and leave to cool overnight in the fridge. Next day when ready to serve, cut into cubes, and fry in a good amount of canola oil in the wok until crispy. Be careful, as this can splash.

Blend all dressing ingredients and place in a non-reactive pan. Bring to a simmer for 5 minutes. Pass through a coarse sieve. Cool.

Arrange pork on a platter with some micro herbs and crispy shallots. Dress with a little of the soy dressing.

Leaving Kerikeri the next morning we are on the last leg of our journey before heading back to Auckland. Our last stop is at Baylys Beach for a couple of nights. With only a short walk to the beach we are off for our last beach swim out of Auckland, and a chance to watch our best beach sunset yet. The next day we are ready to visit the local café in Baylys Beach for dinner.

# THE FUNKY FISH

### 34 Seaview Road, Baylys Beach, RD7
**DARGAVILLE**

### SUPREME

The Funky Fish celebrated its 10th birthday in December 2010, and owner Beth Kelliher has been here since the beginning. She originally created the café with Dave and Kate Northover which was a very happy union, but in 2006 Dave and Kate wanted to retire and so Beth took over ownership. These days she and partner Hiramai Nom are the heart and soul of The Funky Fish.

**Art and music are integral to its vibe;** the art is all local and changes every six to eight weeks. Beth finds at times the view of the art is a real pleasure, while at other times it is not so much to her taste — either way it does its job as a way of giving back to the community. The outdoor area out back has a fantastic mural, part of which was created by a traveller who wanted to leave her mark. Original partner Kate Northover is a very artistic being and is responsible for the interesting toilet and much of the other wall art.

Music is apparent with live music in the garden on Sundays through the summer months. In winter, open microphone nights are a hit as are the quiz nights that keep the locals going. The pool of talent that turns up from the local community never ceases to amaze Beth.

Breakfast is not a feature at The Funky Fish; they tend to concentrate on the lunch and dinner market. Being licensed tends to push towards the later rather than the earlier end of the day. The food is simple, fresh and yummy, and the atmosphere casual, making it a perfect place for us after a day sightseeing.

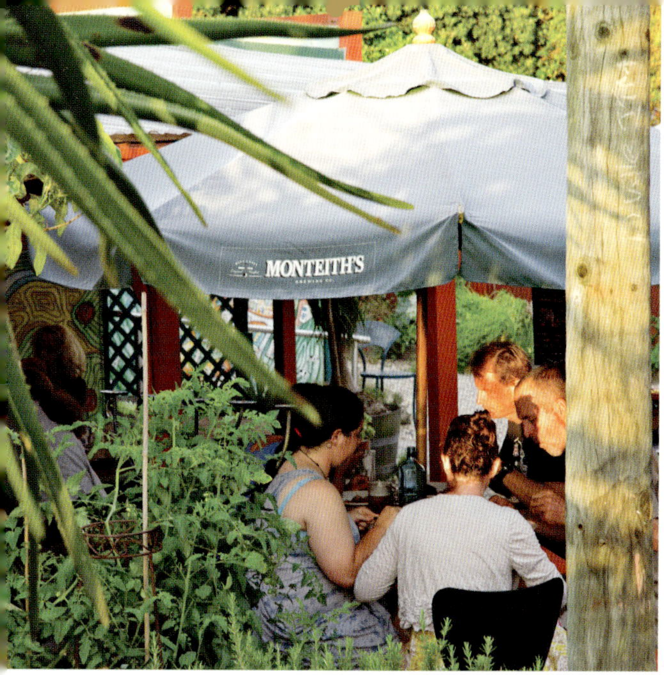
MONTEITH'S

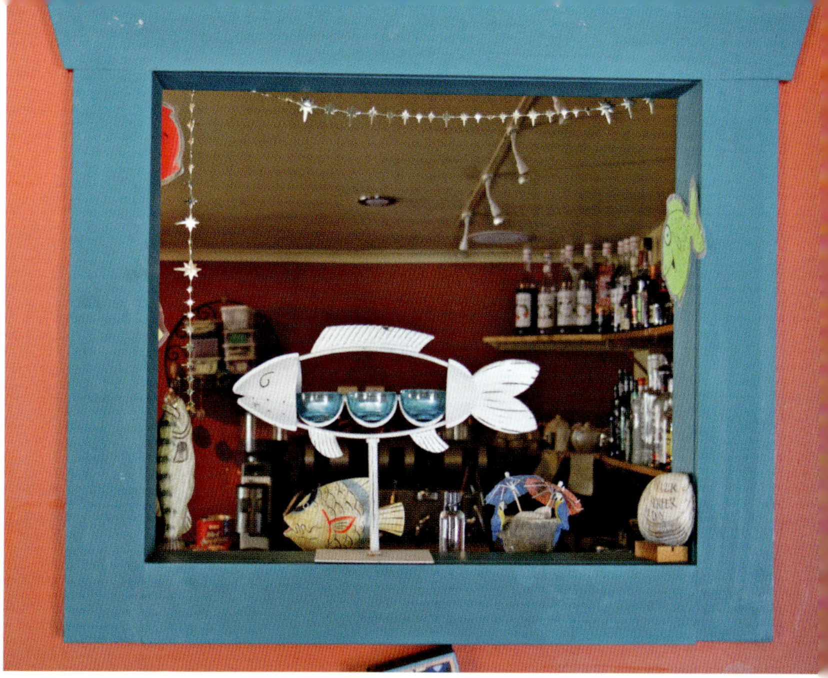

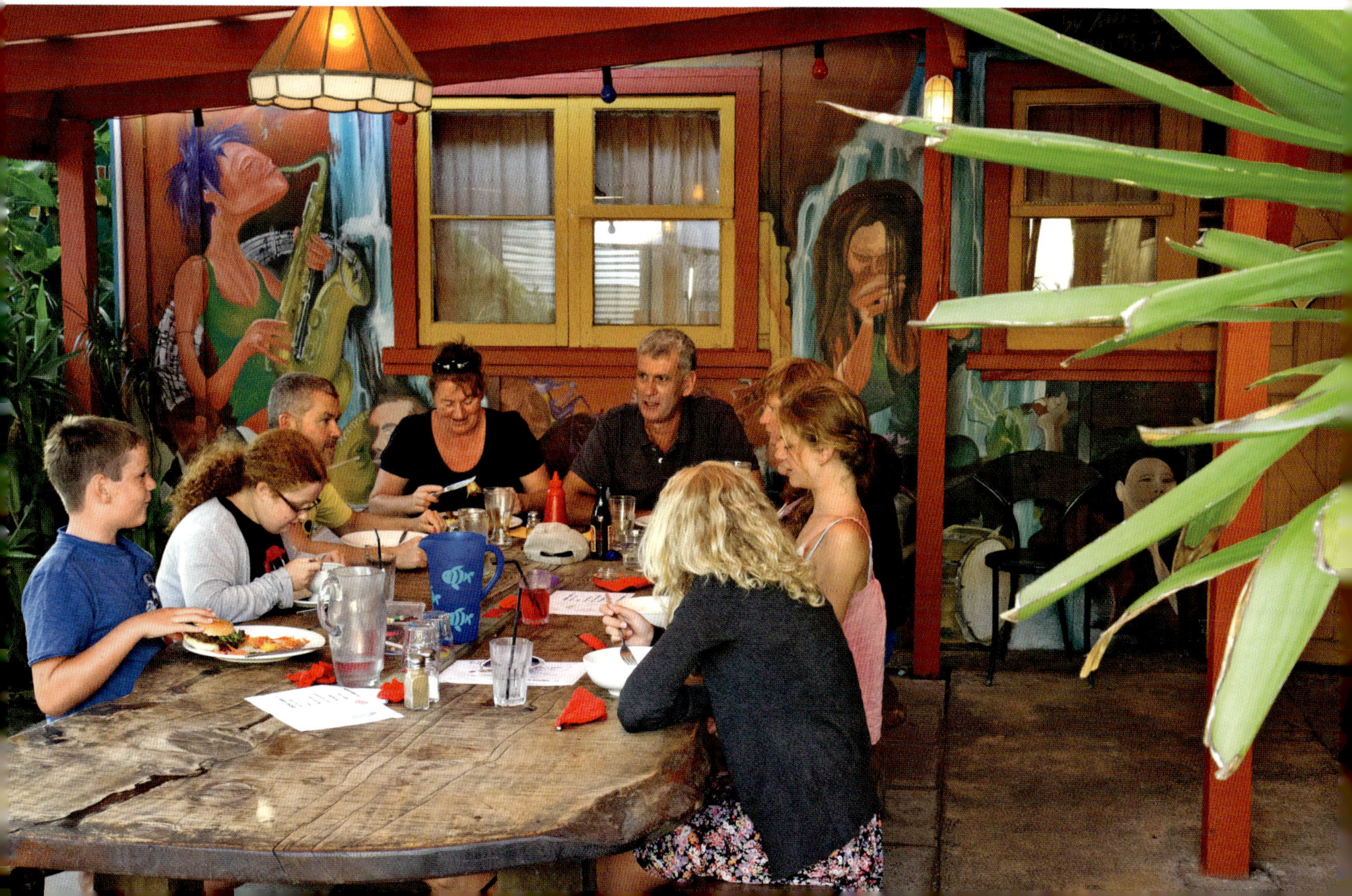

We wake up the following morning feeling a little depressed. We are going home and the road trip is almost over. We would do it all again in a heartbeat, but school calls and the book has to be written. Our last stop before seeing the Auckland suburbs again is Orewa. A seaside beach resort town, it's only a stone's throw from the Waiwera Thermal Resort, a great place to stop for a soak while the kids do the slides. From here you can nip over the hills and have a meal at the well-hidden Walnut Cottage Café.

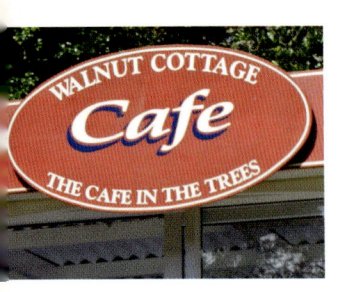

# WALNUT COTTAGE CAFÉ

**498 Hibiscus Coast Highway**
**OREWA**

### KARAJOZ

Just as you arrive in Orewa, on the right you will find the café. It is on the main highway and yet tucked back off the road in a grassy, tree-lined haven. The café is right next to the historic Orewa House, and if you were in need you could have a massage, baby and coffee all in the same location — midwife and massage therapist are some of the businesses there.

In October 2006 Klaus, Kerstin and Yves Zelles took over the café, having been searching for a business since arriving in New Zealand from Germany. It has been an uphill battle trying to overcome a reputation that had been in decline over the years. They still have people commenting that 'the new owners' have improved the café greatly.

The food has a European feel, with everything other than the Swiss Bakery bread created on site. The menu is extensive and we are particularly pleased to see a varied children's menu. The kids are well catered for with an outdoor playground, and often on a sunny weekend day a bouncy castle is added. A single-parent goose family is in residence and often comes to visit from the creek that runs behind the café.

**Solid, simple and quality are the words that best describe the Walnut Cottage Café.** You will find touches of home that make life easier, such as the mobile above the nappy change table and the condiment basket that magically appears once you are seated. If you are located within range of Orewa, Walnut Cottage Café makes a great destination for the day.

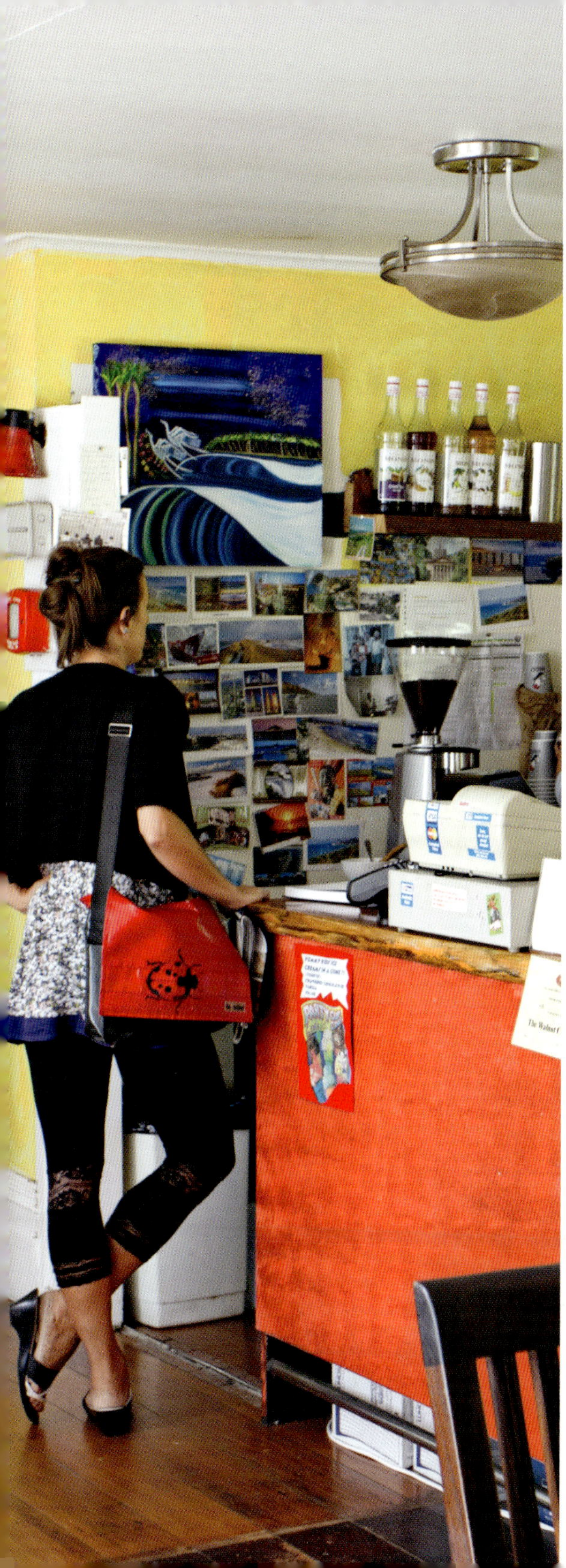

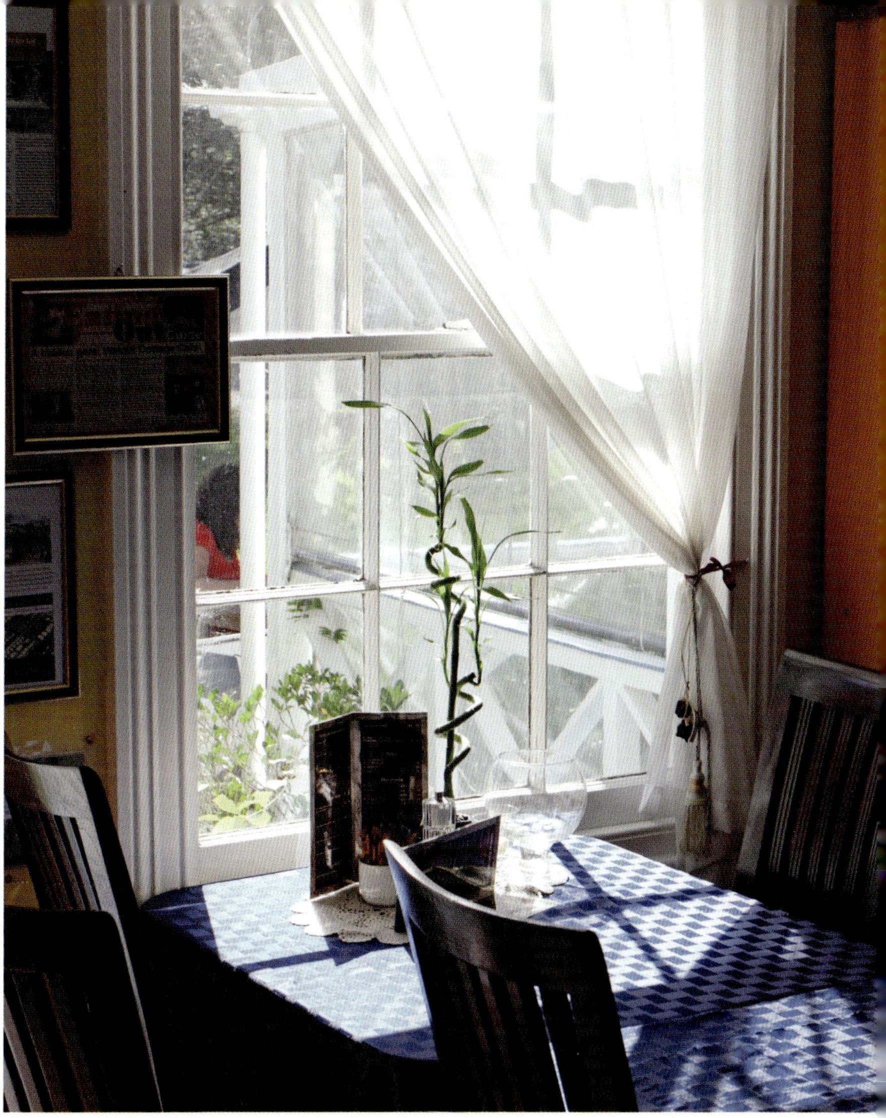

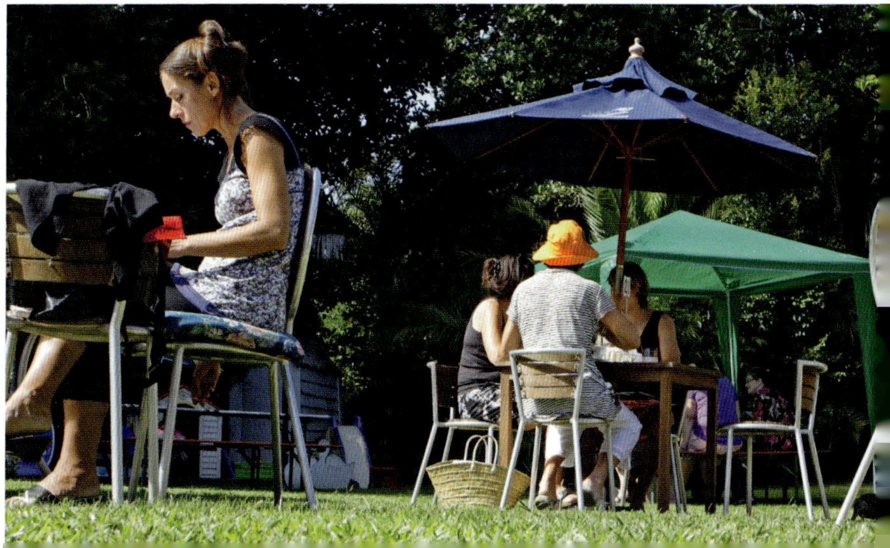

Auckland is a large city with diverse communities, giving many character café choices. There are too many to include all of them here, so we will tell you of our favourites and feature four of them. The Kauri Gum Store in Riverhead is like an old museum, with good food and coffee (look out for the skeleton). The elegance of the Takapuna Beach Café and Store in Takapuna is sublime, and it's right on the beach. The guys in Jukes Espresso in Onehunga have the biggest community spirit we have come across, and Queenie's Lunchroom in Freemans Bay offers fantastic coffee with style to match. Like the rest of New Zealand, Auckland is defined by its different beaches; Pt Chev in central Auckland is not as well known as Mission Bay, but it has a nice beach, a new playground and is great at high tide. Before you hit the beach, make a stop at the station.

# GARNET STATION CAFÉ

**85 Garnet Road, Westmere**
**AUCKLAND 1022**

## CHIASSO

Girls, girls, and a girlie spirit — that's how Niki describes the Garnet Station Café. We have included it because of its feminine vibe that you don't often find, and we both like it. The character and the flow of service all go to give that rhythm that is of the lovely feminine kind. It is also not too central, being just a little out of the CBD yet still quick to get to.

Garnet Station is not a big café, **it is a place for conviviality and to make friends as you chat to your neighbour.** If you notice the lamp shades, co-owner Verity George made them from old rolls of bamboo paper she had been carrying around for years. There is a real organic bent, and with all this evolution we wonder what will happen next. Verity and Lisa Prager bought the building in 2007, when it was a dump. It had been unloved for over 30 years, but they brought it back from the brink of dilapidation.

Lisa and Verity call this an evolving business because they didn't even know it was going to be a café when they started out. They listened to the local community and before you knew it Garnet Station Espresso Bar was making great coffee. They soon added small treats, and while we are there this has grown to include pies and sandwiches. There are Spanish and Italian influences, as can be seen by Gaudi-inspired wrought iron gates outside. In case you don't know, Gaudi is the famous architect of Barcelona.

Garnet Station

Heading west our next stop has to be Piha, one of Auckland's best-known beaches for surf and the place of Lion Rock. It takes many windy roads surrounded in bush to get to Piha, but this is our last chance on this road trip to enjoy the surf — the coffee had better be good.

# PIHA CAFÉ

**20 Seaview Road, Piha**
**WAITAKERE CITY**

### SANTOS

Travelling down a steep, windy, narrow road you are transported into a sleepy world that is one of New Zealand's meccas for surfing. For a long time the only buildings at Piha that serviced the public were the caravan park, a small library and the local shop for supplies and the postal service. Next door was a Telecom exchange which later took over the role of Post Office as well. But a fire in 2004 left it boarded up while Telecom decided what to do with it. Eventually they put it up for tender, and here is where the fun begins.

Five lads who had played rugby together and loved Piha thought this would make a great place for a café. Andy, Rich, Chris, Marc and Dave set up the Preserve Piha Company and started the ball rolling to make their dream come true. But with all good dreams, there is always opposition.

Opposition argued that having a commercial café would increase traffic, change the face of Piha and eventually lead to another Gold Coast. It was progress versus heritage, with both sides having an argument. Three years later, with one of the five dropping out, and a bitter battle over, consent was finally approved.

The question on our minds is, has Piha changed with the opening of the café? It is late morning, and as we walk along the beach we watch a man practising with his taiaha. We watch, mesmerised by his fluid movements, and the sense of Piha timelessness freshens our souls.

**The Piha Café is one of those special gems, made with beautiful natural woods, and featuring little details that make the difference, such as the espresso handles as door handles.** It blends in without needing to make a show of itself; you can easily drive past and not even see it. This is the essence of Piha, special without needing to tell everyone. The Piha Café is a character café with an interesting history, born out of controversy and determination. It provides a wonderful backdrop to the ruggedness of a great New Zealand West Coast beach.

And now a visit to the North Shore. Across the road from Takapuna Grammar School down a side street is our next café. You would be forgiven for thinking that this is not the place for a good café, but this little gem has quite a reputation.

# LITTLE AND FRIDAY

### 43C Eversleigh Road
### TAKAPUNA

#### SUPREME

There are some of us who love to eat food, others who love to create it. Kim Evans is the second type of person, almost fanatically so, and this is at the heart of Little and Friday. Growing up, her mum was a home economics teacher and baking was a familiar event. By the time she was a young woman at art school she was baking cakes and slices to exchange for art supplies. After leaving art school she worked in a cake shop in Oxford Street, Sydney. There she learnt about making amazing corporate cakes, such as a scale replica of an ocean liner.

When Kim came back to New Zealand she opened Ice It in Devonport and began selling her cakes. Having no formal cooking training, she watched other chefs and learned. She kept Ice It for five years until she decided to move to Christchurch. Things didn't work out, and she returned to Auckland broke and with a need to make money.

Take it to the people, and the people will come. This is one of Kim's philosophies, and it wasn't long before she was selling up to 200 bacon and egg pies at the Takapuna markets, working out of her commercial kitchen in Eversleigh Road, a suburban back street in Takapuna. She was soon sick of being stuck inside a kitchen, so stripped away the windows and opened to the world. And so Little and Friday was born — so called because it was small and she was only open Fridays.

Everything here is baked fresh the same day; the pies don't come out until 11 am. The food is organic, free range and there's no microwave. Kim strongly believes that it's not all about money, but about creating food that is alive and ethically correct. She works from early in the morning to late at night, and all the family pitch in as well. **One of those special gems tucked away that you fall in love with when you find it,** and now open seven days.

## LITTLE AND FRIDAY'S **DOUGHNUTS**

**8 g dried yeast**
**¾ cup milk**
**1 egg**
**⅛ cup sugar**
**2 ½ cups flour**
**1 teaspoon salt**
**50 g butter, melted**

Dissolve the yeast in the milk, adding the egg and stirring well to combine. Place the remaining ingredients except the butter into a mixing bowl. Mix on low speed, adding the liquid. When the sticky dough forms, stop the mixer, scrape down the bowl then increase the speed to medium and mix until a soft shiny dough forms that pulls clean away from the bowl. Add melted butter and mix well to combine.

Cover bowl and allow dough to prove for 60 minutes until increased in volume by 50–75%. Mix dough lightly then spread onto a floured board and cut out 5 cm circles with a cookie cutter.

Heat saucepan of oil to 180°C and drop in the dough, cook until dark in colour and let cool. Use a skewer or 'wrong end' of a teaspoon to make a cavity in the doughnut and fill with whipped cream and raspberry jam. Roll in icing sugar and bliss will follow.

You can't talk about Alleluya without mentioning Millers Coffee. Tucked behind Karangahape Road in Cross Street, Craig Miller has been doing espresso since the 1980s and is one of the early coffee pioneers in Auckland. He is a purist at heart, and if you want a 'bloody good espresso' Millers café is the place to visit. But we can't end a café journey without heading to Alleluya, which also has Millers. Nestled in Auckland's oldest arcade on K Road, this café is possibly the city's oldest.

# ALLELUYA

**179/183 Karangahape Road (St Kevin's Arcade)**
**AUCKLAND CENTRAL**

## MILLERS

Imagine it's the early 1920s, we have won the war and life has somewhat returned to normal. Electric trams are everywhere and the motor car is on the increase in Auckland. The walk from Queen Street to K Road along Myers Park has improved with the building of St Kevin's Arcade in 1924. There is talk of making pedestrians keep to the left on pavements; meanwhile the city is about to head into a depression. In this era a new shop opened in the arcade called The Iona Tea Rooms. It lasted for around 10 years and then became the Penrith Tea Rooms, and then a series of coffee lounges. Later reincarnations did not do well and by the early 1990s the owner closed her doors.

Serendipity strikes again — the same day the coffee shop closed Peter Hawkesby, then in his mid-40s, had just touched down from spending 10 years in Tokyo. Peter had little money but had always wanted a place in St Kevin's Arcade; it was an area he was familiar with, having grown up locally. For Peter K Road is a more 'real' place than Ponsonby, and the chance to get the coffee shop in the arcade was a dream come true.

Peter obtained the lease in October 1994 and demolished what was there. With the help of some great friends it was rebuilt and open again in December. Alleluya — the birth of one of Auckland's most original cafés.

Peter's philosophy is that a café must be fun and have a sense of community. Today some of his original staff are still here, and those that aren't have gone on to become baristas in places as far away as Berlin, creating a bit of Alleluya as they go. There is a real sense of history, and the café still serves Millers coffee, exactly as it did in 1994. People have met here, got engaged, married, and now come back with their kids.

In the 1920s people used to pop into a friend's place; you didn't need to ask, there was always time to say hello. In these fast times there is a refreshing atmosphere at Alleluya of this pop-in culture being maintained. When we try to organise a meeting with Peter he says, 'just pop in after two, I'll be here.' **The place is unhurried, full of character and a real slice of the old Auckland.** We think it's fantastic that Peter has the wisdom to follow his desires and turn his dream into reality.

# WHERE TO NEXT?

Well, that's the end of our journey around New Zealand's character cafés, and for us the most amazing experience. To finish, we look to the future and how the world of coffee might be. Flat White is the name of a café in Soho, London. It was set up by James from the Lyttelton Coffee Company in 2006, after a friend from Australia was lamenting how he couldn't get a good coffee in London. One thing led to another to create the Flat White Café. It struggled for the first year as everyone over there is used to the chains such as Starbucks. But expats got behind it and it wasn't long before it starting doing well. The rumour going around is Starbucks are pulling out; in Auckland two stores have closed.

By the time you read this book New Zealand will have probably become the global standard for a café, and the rest of the world will be at our doorstep wanting to franchise us. Typical isn't it? We taught people how to fly, gave the world the power of the atom, and now we show them how to drink coffee.

# ACKNOWLEDGEMENTS

## HONDA NEW ZEALAND ODYSSEY

Whether on an extended adventure or an intellectual quest, the Honda Odyssey delivers the solution for those who enjoy a dynamic sports sedan, need versatility and don't want to compromise. With its Takasu track heritage and leading design, the Odyssey gives you the best choice of driveability combined with seven full-size seats. And it's easily configured to take all your gear as well. Meaning the drive is not only satisfying for you, it's a great journey for everyone.

## BUSINESS NETWORK INTERNATIONAL (BNI)

The ultimate business stimulant? Ever since the first coffee house opened in England in 1652, Western business men and women have gathered around their bowls of coffee to network — passing referrals, talking opportunities and making deals. Coffee's business roots run deep, and nothing has changed. Today, more than 2,800 BNI business men and women throughout New Zealand gather in cafés and other venues over breakfast and a cup of coffee . . . talking opportunities, passing referrals and making deals.

BNI is a structured business referral network that helps members build strong business relationships with each other. The premise of BNI is 'Givers Gain' — if you help other people build their businesses with good quality referrals, they will reciprocate. As Rudy Kokx of BNI Probiz says, 'BNI is now responsible for 80–90 per cent of my business. Besides the referrals I get through the group, I find it a perfect way not to go crazy working by myself the whole week. The help I get from members has been amazing and that was something I never expected to find. I love BNI!' Visit www.bni.co.nz to find out more and discover if growing your business through referrals is for you — we'll keep the coffee jug warm.

## MOA — THE STORE
### 413 Richmond Road
### GREY LYNN

A constant that runs through the creation of our first book, and this one, are the individuals who create beauty and experience as a result of their passion. The Moa Store is no exception and has always been a favourite place for Niki to browse and dream. The clothes are made by New Zealand designers who are committed to quality, beauty and providing these to New Zealand women. For this project Niki was one of those women and she enjoyed every moment of wearing her Moa dresses.

Kia Ora Whaea,
Nga mihi whakawhetai ki a koutou katoa mo o koutou taonga tino aataahua. Ka tino iti taku ngakau i to koutou oha mai . . . nga mihi nga mihi nga mihi atu ra.

## AUCKLAND CAMERA CENTRE
### 646 New North Road, Morningside, AUCKLAND

*Phone 09 849 4920, 0800 624 522; Fax 09 815 0807
Email: aucklandcamera@clear.net.nz
www.aucklandcamera.com*

Why should you buy from these guys? They know about cameras, are passionate about photography, and you will get a level of expertise the superstores won't give you. If that's not enough, take a look at their prices. It's an easy choice really.

# THE ODYSSEY EXPERIENCE

When we were planning this road trip we both agreed we were not prepared to drive around the whole country with three kids in one back seat. The bickering and cramped space would drive us all insane. The Honda Odyssey had enough seats for seven comfortably and it had good luggage space as well. We met with Honda New Zealand and before we knew it were driving around the country in a Honda Odyssey. This is our chance to tell you what it was like.

Driving a Honda Odyssey is like driving a car — it feels good on the road, it handles well, and there's plenty of power when you need it. Although it is a long car, the length only seems to make the handling better.

We often felt like we were cocooned from the world in a safe bubble, with all seats having a wide field of vision to enjoy the beautiful New Zealand scenery. Dual air conditioning kept us all comfortable, and six CDs and iPod input gave us great sounds.

But it's the little things that really made the difference, such as the ease with which the far back seats can be put forward to get out, automatic lights and an electric driver's seat which made changing driving positions easy. And there are many nooks and crannies that always seemed just right for the things we put in the car.

The only thing we regretted with the Odyssey was giving it back.

# HUHTAMAKI

When you're driving down the road enjoying your takeaway coffee from your favourite café, the company that made the cup for you is probably Huhtamaki. What makes Huhtamaki special is their innovation and attention to quality while keeping the manufacturing local, not an easy task these days. These guys have been in Henderson since 1962, making paper hot cups since the 1970s and now supply roasters across the country.

Roasters are very passionate about making the best roasts and want the very best for their cafés. This means the best takeaway cup, without paying an arm and a leg for it. Huhtamaki has been able to do this while using only paper from purpose-grown sustainably managed cup board forests.

Huhtamaki has kept the Kiwi tradition of being great innovators alive, having developed the double wall cup in 2003 and the one-size-fits-all lid in 2008. What will they do next? Build in a sensor that keeps your coffee at the optimal temperature? Quality, innovation and competitive pricing from a local manufacturer, that's what Huhtamaki is all about.

# THE PLACES WE VISITED

During our trip many places became involved with our adventure by providing us with either free accommodation, or free adventure expeditions and experiences to keep the kids happy. Without their help our trip would have been considerably more work than it was. Thanks to all of you, it was great to have so many people believe in what we were doing and help make it that little bit easier . . .

**WOODLYN PARK**
1177 Waitomo Valley Road, RD7
Otorohanga
07 878 6666

**BLUE DUCK LODGE**
3555 Oio Rd
Owhanga
07 895 6276

**THE LEGENDARY BLACK WATER RAFTING CO.**
Waitomo
0800 228 464

**BELT ROAD SEASIDE HOLIDAY PARK**
2 Belt Road, New Plymouth
0800 804 204

**WHANGANUI RIVER TOP 10 HOLIDAY PARK**
460 Somme Parade, Whanganui
0800 272 664

**SPIRIT OF THE RIVER**
1018 Para Para Road, Upokongare
Wanganui 0800 5388687

**INTERISLANDER**
Picton and Wellington Port
0800 802 802

**WHALE WATCH KAIKOURA NEW ZEALAND**
Whaleway Station Road
0800 655 121

**RIVERSONG COTTAGES AND MASSAGE**
30 Fairfax Street, Murchison
03 523 9011

**MOTUEKA TOP 10 HOLIDAY PARK**
10 Fearon Street, Motueka
0800 66 88 35

**NEW RIVER BLUEGUMS B&B HOMESTAY**
985 Main South Road, New River, Greymouth
03 762 6678

**FRANZ JOSEF TOP 10 HOLIDAY PARK**
2902 Franz Josef Highway
03 752 0735

**A J HACKETT BUNGY**
Cnr Camp and Shotover Street, Queenstown
0800 286 4958

**DART RIVER JET SAFARIS**
Mull Street, Glenorchy
0800 327 853

**TSS EARNSLAW TRIP**
Real Journeys, Queenstown
0800 65 65 01

**MONARCH MOTEL**
633 Tay Street, Invercargill
0800 287 666

**THE POUNAWEA MOTOR CAMP**
Parklane, Pounawea, Owaka
03 415 8483

**LAKE OHAU LODGE**
2295 Lake Ohau Road, Ohau
03 438 9885

**THE COTTAGE**
Waipawa, Hawke's Bay
06 858 4997

**WAINUI WHITE WAVES**
Wainui, Gisborne
06 863 2996

**MALFROY MOTOR LODGE**
51 Malfroy Road, Rotorua
07 346 8053

**ARIAS COTTAGE AND CABIN**
396 Clayton Road, Rotorua
07 348 0790

**MACYS MOTOR INN**
Cnr 11th Ave and Edgecumbe Road, Tauranga
0800 006 2297

**SOUTHPACIFIC ACCOMMODATION**
245 Port Road, Whangamata
07 865 9580

**THE ALLAMBEE BED AND BREAKFAST**
1680 Tiki Road, Coromandel
07 866 8011

**GRAFTON COTTAGES AND CHALETS**
304 Grafton Road, Thames
07 868 9971

**KERI KERI COURT MOTEL**
93 Kerikeri Road, Kerikeri
0800 53745374

**BAYLYS BEACH HOLIDAY PARK**
24 Seaview Road, Baylys Beach
0800 Baylys